A 7-SESSION BITE-SIZE BIBLE STUDY THROUGH THE BOOK OF EPHESIANS

WALK IN love

STEPHANIE BEAULIEU
WITH KATHY MORALES

The video sessions were made possible by a generous partnership with the CNBC

Since I became a Christian as a young adult, I have loved women's Bible study. God first laid an idea on my heart years ago. While on a plane to Calgary from Winnipeg, I was reading my Bible, praying and considering all the changes in my life. I was overwhelmed with thankfulness to God, and so grateful for the transforming power of His Word.

As I was reflecting on women I knew, a thought came to my mind: "Just the Word." *If all women, everywhere, could just get into the Word,* they could be transformed. One of the values of the Canadian National Baptist Convention is *"all kinds of churches for all kinds of people."* We are pleased to partner with Stephanie and offer you this bite-size Bible study, an opportunity to get into the word in small, bite-size chunks. I look forward to seeing women connect with the Word and hearing how God uses His Word to transform lives!

Kathy Morales, CNBC Women's Ministry Leader
To learn more, visit http://www.cnbc.ca

About the Author

Stephanie Morales-Beaulieu is a lover and communicator of God's Word and shares that passion online, from the stage, in her living room and anywhere else God opens a door. Bite-size Bible study was birthed out of a heart and a passion to make the transforming power of the Word accessible to those new to Scripture, those overwhelmed by it, and those longing to be transformed by it. She is a born communicator with contagious love and enthusiasm for Jesus. As a wife and mom of three, she shares from her wealth of relatable stories that will inspire you to see everyday life through the lens of truth. She is authentic, funny and you will wish she lived next door.

Connect Online: everydaytruth.ca
Instagram @everydaytruthca

ISBN: 978-1-9995601-1-9

Printed and Bound at Supreme Printing Ltd. in Calgary, Alberta, Canada (3rd Edition)

Cover Photo by Verity Sanders on Unsplash

TABLE OF CONTENTS

GETTING STARTED:

The study guide is designed to be used regularly throughout the six weeks, with Scripture passages, discussion, and personal reflection questions for you to work through.

The more frequently and consistently you are meeting with God in His Word, the more you will get to know Him! The video sessions are short videos that you will watch once per week, which explore even more deeply the material that you will be pondering in your personal study guide.

To get the most out of this study, gather your study materials and keep them together in the place that you will spend your time alone with God each day. I would encourage you to have a hard copy of the Bible, a copy of the study guide, bookmark(s), a pen, pencil and highlighter.

WHAT SHOULD I DO EACH DAY?

The personal study guide is loosely structured to allow for flexibility. You can do one part each day, split it up over multiple days, or do your weekly personal study in one sitting if you prefer. Remember, daily bread is about daily relationship. The more frequently and consistently you are meeting with God in His Word, the more you will get to know Him!

OPTIONAL VIDEO SESSIONS:

This bite-size Bible study also includes seven optional video sessions that will be delivered to your email inbox after you sign up.

1. **Sign up** to receive the video sessions via email at:

   http://everydaytruth.ca/ephesians/

   You will receive video session 1 immediately following email sign up. After that, one video per week will be sent to you automatically.

2. **Watch** Video Session 1 and complete the **Discussion/Reflection Questions** individually, with a friend or small group.
3. **Get Into the Word:** Complete the personal study guide (recommended timeframe is 1 week)
4. **Repeat** for Sessions 2-7

A NOTE FROM STEPHANIE...

Welcome to Get Into the Word. I am so excited you have joined. My prayer is that as you get into the Word, it will get into you. God's Word has the power to change our minds and transform our lives which is just what God wants to do as we study Ephesians together. This study is titled "Walk in Love" based on Ephesians 5:1.The term "walk" is used to describe all of life. It is how you conduct yourself in every single area without exemption or exception.

God's Word declares over and over again the direct relationship between love for God and obedience to God. If we love Him, we will obey Him. I think we often get this backwards. We try to obey Him before we've really fallen in love with Him. This often leads to frustration and failure, or feeling like God is never quite satisfied with your efforts.

How do we get to the place where we truly love Him with everything - where love is our life, not just information we share or a theory we know? Where it's not something we trust only because we've been told or believe in theory but something we have experienced the transforming power of?

God has been stirring this up in my life over the past few years. I found myself in relationships that were far beyond my own ability to love. I was frustrated and failing. What I prayed was this: *"Lord, show me how you've loved me. Show me what I look like through Your eyes so I can love people in the same way."*

When you pray according to His will, buckle in. The way He showed me how He has loved me was and is by showing me the true condition of my heart. He revealed that I wasn't as lovable as I thought. Buried below my good behaviour was a heart plagued by a critical spirit, selfishness, rebellion, judgmentalism, fear, control and much more. When I began to see how unlovable I really was, I saw His love in an amazing new light. As I began to see myself as more broken than I realized, He gave me His perspective to see others as broken and hurting rather than just what was observable on the outside.

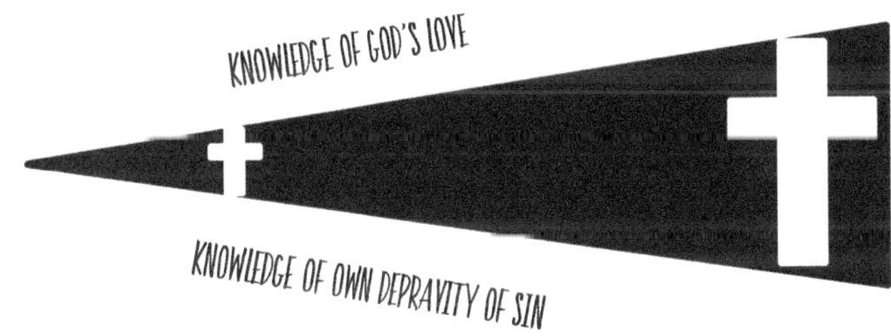

Living a life of love begins with understanding our own depravity, hopelessness, and our need because it leads to a greater understanding of God's love. When we have a high view of ourselves, we see little of our need and I think we experience less of His love. When we begin to understand our great need, our understanding of His love becomes greater. His love never changes. It has always been steadfast and amazing. Our ability to understand and experience His love does.

The divine instruction to walk in love is really to be so aware of God's love for us, that it ignites our love and obedience for Him and impacts every single area of our lives. Nothing is untouched. Nothing is unaffected. It's not something that we experience at church, and then go about our marriages, parenting, work, ministry and lives. It's something that infiltrates every area.

The first three chapters of Ephesians, Paul wants to make sure we know who we are. It's all about our identity.

"The whole of Jesus' teaching is geared to confront and rearrange a person's thinking about identity... The assumption of Jesus' teaching is that the identity he described is the identity people should have, what God intended from the beginning, and that if people see that identity, they will want to choose and can choose that identity and by God's grace grow into it. [i]

If we try to change our conduct without an understanding of who we are in Christ we will be limited because a life of love is a reflection of a loving relationship. It isn't something we can manufacture, it's about a connection. As we grow in our understanding of who we are in Christ, our lives follow suit and increase in love and grace. It is the result of continually realizing what Jesus has done for us, falling at His feet in gratitude and crying out and desiring to respond to Him in whatever way He asks.

The big picture for the beginning of Ephesians is this: A life of love of hinges on my understanding of how I've been loved. We will naturally do what we've experienced. If we have misconceptions about God's love for us, then we will love others with the same perceptions. For example, if I think that God only loves me or is pleased with me when I'm on my best behaviour, then I might be limited to loving others (friends, kids, spouse) when they're "behaving" correctly.

The goal by the end of our study of the first three chapters, is that through the truth God will reveal, that we would be beside ourselves with gratitude. That will position us to respond in obedience to all the instructions in the latter part of the letter.

The big picture for the second half of this study in chapters 4-6 has to do with how we respond.

> *When we make decisions, we typically rely on one of two models: consequences model (weigh the costs and benefits to maximize immediate satisfaction; or the identity model which asks, what kind of person am I? What would someone like me do in this situation? Our identities are so central to the way we make decisions. The consequences model can influence us in the short term but because identity is SO central to how we make decisions, if there is an effort to change not rooted in identity, (or an identity change) it's likely doomed to fail.*[ii]

Once we really start to get it, His love in us begins to take shape in our lives. Paul spends a great deal of time talking about who we are in Christ before telling us how it should take shape in our lives.

Our big picture for the second half of Ephesians is this: A life of love is a reflection of a loving relationship.

Our life conduct and our obedience has everything to do with a present tense relationship with our Lord. Our capacity to obey the specific instructions we see in the second half of Ephesians boil down to the closeness of our current walk with Him. Do I believe who I am in Christ? Am I presently in touch with His love for me? If not, a lot of those instructions move from hard to impossible. But when we abide with Him in His love for us, our lives simply become an overflow of what He's pouring into us.

I want to be known for and remembered as someone who walked in love. I want to pour my life into loving God and loving others the same way Jesus loves me.

What better way to spend your life, than fulfilling the two greatest commandments: to love God, and to love others? Whether it's your spouse, your children, your extended family, your in-laws, your neighbours, I'm willing to bet there's not a shortage of people in your life who need love (with skin on it) in order to really begin to understand God's love for them.

Let's get started! I'm so humbled and thankful to be on this journey with you,

WEEK 1: UNDERSTANDING WHO I AM

A NEW PERSPECTIVE

While driving one day, my toddler daughter was puzzled at the fact that it was sunny, then cloudy, then sunny again as the van travelled underneath the moving clouds.

"Mommy it's cloudy!!! Mommy now it's sunny!!!…. It's cloudy agaaaaiiinnn!!!"

She didn't know what to think and her confusion was genuine. *"Why's it keep changin'?"*

I glanced in the rear view mirror and said, *"The sun is always in the same place. The clouds are just moving and covering it, but it's still shining. We're moving and the clouds are moving so there are times the sun is harder to see than others."*

Then I felt the Lord saying, *the sun is like me, constant and unchanging. I am faithful. Your circumstances, perspective, relationships and emotions are like the clouds. They block you from being able to see me at times, but it doesn't change the truth that I am there. I allow changing weather in your life, but I don't change. I am constant. Your circumstances and seasons are changing just like the passing scenery you're driving by. But in all of it, are you aware that I am here?*

In part one you're going to study who you are and what you have in Christ. God in His grace knows about our spiritual amnesia. We forget who He is, who we are and what He's called us to do. It's too easy to get caught up in merely surviving from day to day. We easily lose sight of eternity.

The enemy is always out to steal, kill and destroy. I've realized that an extremely effective tactic He has used on me is to distract. Cloudy weather hides the reality of the sun. He has successfully distracted me from the fact that Jesus paying for my sins on the cross and God's Spirit living in me combine to create the awesome invitation to life. Not just living. Not just surviving. *Abundant* life. Life to the *full.* (John 10:10)

Walking in love begins with understanding the eternally secure identity change that took place when you trusted in Jesus. Your position and standing before God was instantly and forever changed. This change took place outside of the visible realm as you'll see. The changes we can see and we long for in our lives take a little longer to take shape. Just like the passing clouds, we are easily distracted by our circumstances and our track record, but who we are has been determined by Christ. It is completely secure and is something we continue to grow into as we walk with God.

In part two, you will study Paul's prayer and see how we need continual revelation to grow in our walk with God and grow into our identity.

I'm praying for you as you get into the Word this week!

PART 1: DEFINED BY HIM & COMPLETELY SECURE

READ IT: EPHESIANS 1:1-14 (ESV)

1 Paul, an apostle of Christ Jesus by the will of God, To the saints who are in Ephesus, and are faithful in Christ
Jesus: 2 Grace to you and peace from God our Father and the Lord Jesus Christ. 3 Blessed be the God and Father of
our Lord Jesus Christ, who has blessed us in Christ with every spiritual blessing in the heavenly places, 4 even as he
chose us in him before the foundation of the world, that we should be holy and blameless before him. In love 5 he
predestined us for adoption as sons through Jesus Christ, according to the purpose of his will, 6 to the praise of his
glorious grace, with which he has blessed us in the Beloved. 7 In him we have redemption through his blood, the
forgiveness of our trespasses, according to the riches of his grace, 8 which he lavished upon us, in all wisdom and
insight 9 making known to us the mystery of his will, according to his purpose, which he set forth in Christ 10 as a
plan for the fullness of time, to unite all things in him, things in heaven and things on earth. 11 In him we have
obtained an inheritance, having been predestined according to the purpose of him who works all things according to
the counsel of his will, 12 so that we who were the first to hope in Christ might be to the praise of his glory. 13 In him
you also, when you heard the word of truth, the gospel of your salvation, and believed in him, were sealed with the
promised Holy Spirit, 14 who is the guarantee of our inheritance until we acquire possession of it, to the praise of his
glory.

UNPACK IT:

For this section, feel free to highlight, underline and circle the answers in your own Bible, on the verses above or use the space below:

- Who is responsible for blessing us? (v.3)
- How or through whom are we blessed? (vs.3-5)
- Circle the blessings you have received in Christ. (vs.4-12)
- Put a box around *where* you have received these blessings. (vs. 3)
- Underline the two purposes that are outlined for God's blessing? (vs. 10, 12)

  Hint: look for the word "to" and "so that"
- Who is the guarantee of your inheritance? (vs. 13-14)
- What two events sealed our identity? (v.12)

WORK IT OUT:

The spiritual blessings we have received are better than any earthly gift we could ever ask for. He has the final say over who we are. He gives us what we need to be alive, now and forever. We have the opportunity to live life abundantly and we don't need to wait for heaven for it to unfold.

He chose you. He went looking for you when you weren't looking for Him. He initiated work in your life because He wanted you. Not because you were a solid draft pick, or a good poster girl, but because of His great love. He chose you with good purpose. He set you aside for a particular purpose: to be holy and blameless, meaning, to be set apart and significant and free from anything that would make you unacceptable before Him. He adopted you. He decided ahead of time you'd be His. He planned on giving you a position of dignity as His child despite the fact that you didn't naturally belong.

You are redeemed and forgiven. That means you are never too far out of His reach. He's never ready to write you off or surprised by your behaviour. When He chose you, He knew everything there was to know about you. Nothing that you've done can't be woven into the masterpiece of your life by the master Artist Himself. Sometimes we just want to forget the past and not dig into it or seek healing. However, God can redeem in the present, something that has happened in the past, and use it in the future if we will allow Him to do His work.

Redemption and forgiveness are not rationed out to us. We have been given them according to the riches of His grace. As in, more abundantly than abundant bacon! There was no running out at that buffet and we will never exhaust God's ability to redeem and forgive.

We don't have to guess what His big plan is. He clearly reveals it to us: "*To unite all things to Him.*" His plan was always to bring us home. And He went to serious lengths to make this possible: the Cross.

Please don't miss how this was made possible. Several times in this first chapter you have seen the phrases, "through Jesus" and "in Christ." Our identity was sealed with the Holy Spirit the moment we heard the word of truth, the gospel of salvation, *and* believed in Jesus.

When we are looking at earthly circumstances through an earthly perspective, it's easy to fall into the temptation to believe there is much we haven't received. It's easy to think we are somehow lacking and good things have been withheld from us.

But when we start to understand we are not merely physical beings but we live within an invisible but very real spiritual reality, we see that everything we would ever need has already been provided.

1. When did you first hear the gospel and believe in Jesus? Take a moment to jot a few memories surrounding the moment that identity change took place. What changed that day?

2. What hindrances stand between you and believing and living as though you have *every* spiritual blessing?

3. Tony Evans describes faith this way: *"Acting like it is so, even when it is not so, so that it might be so, simply because God said so."* What would change in your present circumstances if you were to live in a way that reflects the truth of these realities? Marinate in these blessings for a bit and resist the urge to rush through answers!

I believe and receive the fact that I am...	Today, this means that...
chosen (vs. 4)	
adopted (vs. 5)	
made holy and blameless (vs. 4)	
redeemed (vs. 7)	
forgiven (vs.7)	
lavishly given grace (vs. 7)	
given an inheritance (vs. 11)	
sealed with the Holy Spirit (vs.13)	

4. Currently, what spiritual blessings are you most grateful for and why?

PART 2: GROWING INTO MY IDENTITY

READ IT: EPHESIANS 1:15-22

15 For this reason, because I have heard of your faith in the Lord Jesus and your love[f] toward all the saints, 16 I do not cease to give thanks for you, remembering you in my prayers, 17 that the God of our Lord Jesus Christ, the Father of glory, may give you the Spirit of wisdom and of revelation in the knowledge of him, 18 having the eyes of your hearts enlightened, that you may know what is the hope to which he has called you, what are the riches of his glorious inheritance in the saints, 19 and what is the immeasurable greatness of his power toward us who believe, according to the working of his great might 20 that he worked in Christ when he raised him from the dead and seated him at his right hand in the heavenly places, 21 far above all rule and authority and power and dominion, and above every name that is named, not only in this age but also in the one to come. 22 And he put all things under his feet and gave him as head over all things to the church, 23 which is his body, the fullness of him who fills all in all.

UNPACK IT:

- Underline the description of how Paul prays. (v. 16)
- What is the purpose of His prayer? (vs. 17-19)
- What does Paul ask for on behalf of our hearts? Why? (vs. 18)
- What does Paul want us to know? How is it made available to us? (vs. 19-20)
- Where is Christ seated and what is He in charge of? (vs. 20)

WORK IT OUT:

I love that Paul did more than just *think* about the people he ministered to. His thoughts always turned to prayers for them. Prayer makes an impact that our thoughts cannot. In this instance, he prays because he knows there is much more available to us than we may initially realize. I can recall many times in my life where scripture has come alive. There are things we know in theory, but there's nothing quite like when you read truth, and the Spirit testifies within you and you think, wow, now I *really* get this.

Paul prays persistently and without ceasing. He knows we need *continual* revelation from God to grow in our understanding of what we have in Christ so he asks for God's spirit of wisdom and revelation. Read 1 Corinthians 2:11-12 below:

> *"11 For who knows a person's thoughts except the spirit of that person, which is in him? So also no one comprehends the thoughts of God except the Spirit of God. 12 Now we have received not the spirit of the world but the Spirit who is from God, that we might understand the things freely given us by God."*

5. Why do we need the Spirit of God in order to have "knowledge of him"?

Next he asks for the enlightenment of our hearts so that we know the hope we are called to, the riches of our inheritance and the immeasurable great power available. He's asking God to flick the light switch of our hearts on so this truth can settle in. Read Jeremiah 17:9 below:

> *"The heart is deceitful above all things, and desperately sick; who can understand it?"*

6. Why do our hearts need to be enlightened by God?

To have hope means to have favourable and confident expectations. Hebrews 6:19-20a tells us our source of hope, Jesus.

> *"We have this as a sure and steadfast anchor of the soul, a hope that enters into the inner place behind the curtain, where Jesus has gone as a forerunner on our behalf"*

I know with certainty I will need God's wisdom and revelation for the rest of my life to see the truth take shape in my life. The second reason Paul prays for our hearts to be enlightened is so that we will know the *immeasurable great power* available to us who *believe*. If that weren't enough, he gives a little descriptor: the same power that God worked in Jesus to *raise him from the dead.* Can you believe Paul is saying that *same* power is available to us?

Jeremy Camp says it pretty well to so I thought I'd share his take from the song, "Same Power:"

> *"The same power that rose Jesus from the grave, the same power that commands the dead to wake, lives in us, lives in us. The same power that moves mountains when He speaks, the same power that can calm a raging sea lives in us, lives in us, He lives in us."*

The contingency is "to us *who believe.*" Look back at verse 13.

7. What two similar but different words are used in verse 13 and 19?

"Our glorious faith walk began with an act of faith that brought us into relationship with Jesus Christ as our Saviour but it doesn't end there. Having believed in Him, we are called to continue believing all He came to do and say. Tragically, some who have believed in Christ have believed little of Him since. He who began a work in us wants to accomplish far more. God is calling us to leave the passive life bred by a past-tense view of faith and to participate in a present-active-participle believing."[iii]

When my dad was diagnosed with ALS in 2009, our family was blindsided. For me, that season was accompanied by a desperate longing to hear from God in His Word. There are several verses I can call to mind from that season that challenged my faith as I read them. One was from Philippians 4:19.

> *"And my God will meet all your needs according to the riches of his glory in Christ Jesus."*

I had some serious objections for God. What about when I *need* my dad and he's not around? What about when my sister is getting married and he's not there to walk her down the aisle? What about when

I have kids of my own and they don't get to know and play with their Papa? Who will take care of my mom? Surely you know that we still need him!

God heard my cries. In that season, He often responded to me with a question: *Will you trust Me? Will you believe Me now?*

Sometimes a crisis of faith isn't a life altering decision, but a life altering belief. There's nothing quite like when you see something you have believed in faith come to pass in reality.

8. Can you recall a time you've come across a scripture that God was asking you to believe, in a present and active way? What was the result?

I wish I could say I "graduated" from believing that scripture but more recently, I was given the opportunity by God to believe Him in the present. Last summer my husband was particularly busy with some projects outside of our home. Being a stay-at-home-mom, I very much look forward to the weekends where I have someone to double team our little ones with. I was less than thrilled that he was leaving and I let it be known. Upon his departure, feeling sorry for myself was quickly settling in.

During that same time, of course, the Lord was at work, revealing thinking patterns based on lies and obviously not conducive to abundant life. As my thoughts spiraled down a familiar path, the Lord stopped me with another question: *Do you or do you not believe I will supply your every need?*

Don't you love those "convenient" opportunities to believe God? Thankfully, they're often followed by experiencing the reality of the truth you choose to believe. Your present situation may be similar or different than mine but regardless of the specifics, there are always opportunities to choose to believe God, or to be led by our faithless emotions. We need His wisdom, revelation and enlightenment to even begin to identify the areas of our everyday life that we are lacking belief in Him.

The same power that raised the dead is available to those who presently and actively choose to believe God.

9. What is God asking you to believe right now? What action would reflect that you believe His truth? Are you facing any roadblocks to stepping out in faith and believing Him?

WRAP IT UP:

Two years ago at Christmas time, my two year old daughter was very into learning Carols. She was also at the age where she often asked probing questions. One day she was belting out Hark the Herald Angels Sing and she sang, *"G'ory to the newbown kin."* She then paused, looked at me and asked, *"Mummy, what's g'ory"?*

In this instance it seemed inappropriate to say, hold on while I get out my Greek lexicon and exegete the meaning of this word for you. I paused, trying to think of how I could communicate this magnificent concept in toddler terms. All I could manage was, "It means... to recognize God for who He is." She nodded and continued on with her caroling.

As I read in this first chapter of Ephesians that all we've been given might be *to the praise of His glory* I looked at the definition. Have a look below:

> Glory: *The appearance of a person or thing which catches the eye or attracts attention, commanding recognition, looking like something; Equivalent to splendor, brilliance, attracting the gaze which makes it strong*[iv]

Our lives are to catch the eye, attract attention, command recognition because *we look like something.* Better yet, we look like Someone.

I mentioned earlier, we weren't chosen because *our* resumes would make good poster girls for Christianity. But I've concluded that we are intended to be poster girls for His glory because our lives are meant to put Him on display so He can be seen for who He is.

When our identities are determined by our belief in Jesus, when we live securely with the seal and promise of the Holy Spirit, when we continually seek God because we know there is always more to Him than we currently know or have experienced, we put Him on display. Our lives are lived to the praise of His glory. Others will see and know of the forgiveness, redemption and hope that is available.

SUMMARIZE what you have learned regarding who you are in and through Him:

RESPOND by writing out a prayer. Perhaps there are lies you've believed about your identity that you need to confess, and truth you need to agree with. Take a moment to respond to God:

LIVE UP:

Lord, I confess that I don't always live like I believe that You've given me everything. Forgive me for that. Help me to fix my eyes not on what is seen but what is unseen. You've given me every spiritual blessing and I need Your eyes to see this reality. Thank you that You chose me and adopted me. When I feel like no one else wants me, You do. Thank you for forgiving and redeeming me. Not only do You give me a clean slate, but You buy back all of my wrong and have the amazing ability to turn my messes into miracles. Thank you that You are always trying to bring me back. You want me to be united to You. Help me to see You in my present circumstances as I go about this day. I want my life to reflect Your glory. Thank you that You do too. I need You to empty me of me and fill me with Your Spirit so I may be a reflection who You are. Thank you that You've given the Holy Spirit who is my guarantee of what You have promised. Show me where my lack of faith has left me powerless. Show me where I need to believe You. May others see You when they look at me. In the mighty name of Jesus.

---

[i] Klyne Snodgrass," Jesus and a Hermeneutics of Identity," Biblotheca Sacra 168, no. 670 (April-June 2011): 136. (Cited in the Mud

[ii] John Burke, "The Mud and the Masterpiece" p. 73
[iii] Beth Moore, Believing God, p.10-11
[iv] Blueletterbible.org, "Doxa," Strong's 1391

WEEK 2: MERCIFUL LOVE

DEAD IN THE WATER

Last summer I was at the Calgary Stampede with my kids. I returned to the place where I had parked after a long day, a lot of walking, very hot weather, and very tired toddlers. My van was not where I had left it. The "no stopping" sign which I had not noticed before leaving my vehicle was all of a sudden clear and visible. Unfortunately, I was parked one foot in front of the sign making me illegally parked and eligible for towing.

I tracked my van down at the nearest impound lot which was thankfully within walking distance. My car seats were in my impounded vehicle. After waiting at the lot for a long time, my phone died while in the middle of a conversation getting necessary information from my husband so I could get my van released. I asked my fellow offenders if anyone had a charger. Of course, no one did.

There wasn't a thing I could do. It was incredibly frustrating to be sitting next to the electrical outlet, with my dead phone in hand and nothing to connect the two to bring my phone back to life. I sat there helpless, with my dead phone in hand extremely aware that there was nothing I could do to save myself.

Paul ends off chapter 1 with great news about what we have been given in Christ, the great power available to us, and the position we now have before God. Then he opens chapter 2 with a big humbling reminder of where we have come from.

It matters that we get this because we tend to love based on how we perceive we have been loved. As we saw in week 1, we tend to define others by how we ourselves feel defined. Walking in love should flow from what we have received and experienced. Take a moment and pause. Ask God to make this truth come to life for you as you study this week.

As we are better filled with an understanding of how we are loved, walking in love will be the overflow of hearts that are transformed by His great grace and mercy.

PART 1: NOT ABOUT ME

READ IT: EPHESIANS 2:1-3

1And you were dead in the trespasses and sins
2 in which you once walked, following the course of this world, following the prince of the power of the air, the spirit that is now at work in the sons of disobedience—
3 among whom we all once lived in the passions of our flesh, carrying out the desires of the body and the mind, and were by nature children of wrath, like the rest of mankind.

UNPACK IT:

Highlight, underline and circle the answers in your own Bible, or in the space above.

- Underline the descriptors Paul uses for the condition you were in when God chose to save you.

Paul says you were without life in trespasses and sins. Look at the two definitions below:

> *"Paraptoma" (trespasses): to fall beside or near something; a lapse or deviation from truth;*[v]
>
> *"Hamartia" (sins): to miss the mark; to miss or wander from the path of uprightness and honour;*[vi]

There are many ways we can deviate from the truth. Some ways are obvious, others remain invisible inhabitants of our hearts and minds. When we deviate from the truth, miss the mark or wander from the path of uprightness, the result is the same: separation from Life. Paul says we have *all* been there. It might be easy or difficult to identify *how* you've been dead in your trespasses and sins depending on what your measuring stick is. If you reduce living in the passions of your flesh and carrying out the desires of the body and mind to behaviour and outward actions, it can be easy to gloss over.

But what about the invisible? Feeling frozen by fear? Plagued by guilt? Hindered by greed? Coloured with anger? Captivated by needing control or to be right? Gripped by feeling invisible or lacking validation? Addicted to affirmation or pleasing people? Fear of failure or being found out? There can be many areas of our lives difficult to see or admit but equally causing a lack of life in our spirit.

WORK IT OUT:

We were all in the same boat: spiritually dead and unable to save ourselves. Regardless of our upbringing, whether our struggles are observable or invisible, how put together or messy we appear, there was nothing we could do to connect ourselves to the source of Life. We were completely separated from Life Himself. We had nothing to offer, nothing to bring, nor had we accomplished anything good. No matter what our outward struggles, whether our sins are observable, or buried in the depths of our hearts, whether we've been a Christian for days or decades, whether our sins are socially acceptable or not, our salvation has nothing to do with our resume, behaviour or track record. Salvation is a gift from God.

Thankfully, one of the best uses of the word "but" in scripture is coming soon. But before we get there, we need a reality check. I spent many years unaware of my own neediness because outward behaviour and effort were my measuring stick. I was saved as a young child and though my mother can attest to a great deal of disobedience within my young, stubborn nature, I didn't see myself as a child of wrath. I was well-disciplined (thank you mom and dad) and I learned early that avoiding bad behaviour made life easier for everyone, namely me. It's not that I believed I was the exception to truth, but I had difficulty identifying with Paul's description here.

1. What makes it easy or difficult for you to identify with Paul's description of your condition: dead in trespasses and sin, disobedient, carrying out the desires of the flesh and by nature a child of wrath?

2. Do you struggle with disobedience in more invisible or observable ways? Why?

If we aren't careful, good behaviour can be confused with being the reason for our identity and salvation. This entanglement in our thinking might leave us thinking we are in better shape than we really are, and that we aren't desperate in our need for God's saving grace. We aren't always aware of our own neediness, but it's absolutely necessary that we are.

> *"Spiritual poverty is about living in reality. A good way to understand this is to think of spiritual poverty as experiencing our state of incompleteness before God. This can be due to weaknesses, unfulfilled needs, emotional injuries and hurts at the hands of others, and our own immaturities and sins. It has to do with the parts of us that are not as they should be and that we cannot repair in our own strength. When people experience at a deep level their neediness, incompleteness, and dependency—the way they actually are—they are often overwhelmed.... Yet Jesus calls this a "blessed" condition because it helps us get closer to our God. Our state of incompleteness drives us outside of ourselves to God as the source of healing and hope."*[vii]

I clearly remember the season of life when God began to bring me face to face with the true condition of my heart. It wasn't fun. In fact, it was downright depressing. There were lots of tears shed over sin that had silently inhabited my heart for decades. There was a lot of wondering how God could love me and why He would use me in light of what I was discovering.

Thankfully, He didn't leave me in the place of despair though He did let me soak in it for a while. It was humbling and good for me. The good news is I encountered His love in a very real way following that season.

3. Ask God to begin showing you your true state of spiritual poverty. This may take some time so feel free to come back to this question. Ask Him to show you where you need healing. What has he revealed?

My prayer is that you are increasingly aware of your neediness before God and that your need drives you into His loving arms to experience His healing and hope.

PART 2: BECAUSE OF HIMSELF

READ IT: EPHESIANS 2:4-9

4 But God, being rich in mercy, because of the great love with which he loved us, 5 even when we were dead in our
trespasses, made us alive together with Christ—by grace you have been saved— 6 and raised us up with him
and seated us with him in the heavenly places in Christ Jesus, 7 so that in the coming ages he might show the
immeasurable riches of his grace in kindness toward us in Christ Jesus. 8 For by grace you have been saved through
faith. And this is not your own doing; it is the gift of God, 9 not a result of works, so that no one may boast.

UNPACK IT:

- Underline what God did on our behalf (v.5-6, 8)
- Circle the description of why He did it (v.4, 7)
- Where has He seated us and with whom? (v.6)
- How are we saved? Why are we saved this way? (v.8-9)

WORK IT OUT:

Sometimes we think that God is sitting on the throne waiting to pounce and punish. It's our natural tendency to think we're going to get what we deserve. This is the great scandal of the gospel. We don't get what we deserve. God being rich in mercy withheld his wrath from us, and unleashed it on His perfectly holy Son on the cross in our place. It's not fair. Jesus lived the life we should've lived, and died the death we deserved to die. I don't think we're able to fully fathom what we deserve because of our sin.

4. How do you perceive God? As being rich in mercy? A harsh judge waiting to punish? Someone who's never satisfied with you or your efforts?

Whenever I hear a verse or spiritual insight on a topic on multiple occasions within in a short period of time, I'm convinced God is trying to get something important through to me. In four short verses Paul manages to drive this point home with three mentions of the word grace. In case we still haven't quite got it, Paul specifies this is *not* your own doing. Then again, says it's a gift and then one more time for good measure, states it is *not* a result of works. Clearly, he was trying to drive home a point. Why is it so important that we understand this grace gift?

When we forget the grace that God has given us, both to save us and to continually walk in, we are at risk of a few things.

First of all, we are vulnerable to pride. Anytime I think I had something to do it with, I compromise grace. Read the definition of grace below:

> Grace (from the Greek word—charis): absolute freeness of the lovingkindness of God to men finding its only motive in the bounty and freeheartedness of the Giver; unearned and unmerited favor; *Charis* stands in direct antithesis to *erga*, works, the two being mutually exclusive. God's grace affects man's sinfulness and not only forgives the repentant sinner, but brings joy and thankfulness to him. In contrast to *charis* stands *eleos,* mercy, which is concerned not with sin itself as *charis*, but with the misery brought upon the sinner as a consequence of sin." [viii]

5. What stood out to you most from the definition of grace?

Grace isn't only the springboard for salvation but it's the reality that we continually walk in. We learned in chapter 1 that we have redemption and forgiveness *according to the riches of His grace*. We need both on a continual basis. If we ever think we are operating independently of grace it's purely an illusion. This, like so many other spiritual truths is easy to know in theory but harder to live out as we work out our salvation with fear and trembling (Philippians 2:12).

6. How can you live with the awareness that all in your life is grace? Is it easy to leave grace at your conversion?

A second risk we face is feeling disdain towards those who aren't where we think they should be rather than showing mercy:

When God teaches me something, often I wonder why everyone doesn't have the same revelation or conviction. He gently reminds me, I *just* told you that and don't forget it took you *years* to grasp it.

God who is rich in mercy towards us, longs for us to be merciful toward His people. (Matthew 9:12-14). In order to live as a vessel of His mercy and grace, we need to let Him first pour it into our lives so it can be poured out. He has to fill us with grace before our lives can spill grace.

7. If someone were to observe your life, would they find that you are spiritually alive and overflowing with grace (v.5)? What evidence might they find of the Holy Spirit's working?

Lastly, we are vulnerable to doubting God's work and faithfulness in our lives. In the Old Testament, God commanded His people to remember what He had done for them. In difficult times, our autopilot often follows our emotions, our fears and our questions. If we are not intentional about recalling God's faithfulness to us in the past, we can easily miss the opportunity to connect with Him in our present difficulty.

8. Read Psalm 106. Summarize the consequences the Israelites faced because of forgetting what God had done (v.14-39).

9. Have you experienced similar consequences when you have forgotten what God has done for you? Describe below.

10. Though they faced the consequences of their choices, what was God's ultimate response? (v.43-46). What was His response motivated by? (v. 45).

Isn't that a beautiful truth? "For *their* sake, He remembered His covenant and ***out of His great love,*** He relented. He caused all who held them captive to show them mercy" (Psalm 106:45-46). Look back at the difference between grace and mercy explained at the end of the grace definition on page 22. *Grace affects our actual sinful nature whereas mercy is extended for the alleviation of the consequences of our sin.*[ix]

Because of His great love, He spared the Israelites from experiencing the full weight of the consequences of their sin and I'm so thankful His rich mercy extends toward us as well. He knows we cannot stand under the weight our guilt, shame and sin causes us. He's not looking upon us with angry crossed arms saying *I told you so!* He has compassion for the misery sin brings *even when* we bring it upon ourselves.

There was a time where sinful behaviour in myself and others made me feel only frustration, but now more than that, I find it heartbreaking. When I see someone return to an old way or habit that I know is going to end up in the same hurt, disappointment, and guilt, my heart hurts. I know God desires abundant life that the struggle with sin will never give. My heart longs for us to believe Him!

We of course still experience consequences but because of His great mercy, not the full extend. Instead, He makes us alive together with Christ and he has seated us with Him in heavenly places. This was the necessary solution for being dead in our transgressions: a spiritual resurrection with Christ that infused life.

11. How have you seen the grace of God (affects and forgives our sin) and the mercy of God (alleviating the consequences of sin) at work in your own life?

PART 3: WITH PURPOSE

READ IT: EPHESIANS 2:10

10 For we are his workmanship, created in Christ Jesus for good works, which God prepared beforehand, that we should walk in them.

UNPACK IT:

- Circle or underline: What/who are you? Why were you created? What is your responsibility?
- Personalize this verse in the space below replacing the "we" with I and your name

WORK IT OUT:

His Workmanship: When God saved you, He began the lifelong process of restoring you to the original art work He had in mind before you were born. He can see the end at the beginning. That masterpiece is a person who could live boldly and confidently in His continual presence, empowered by His unlimited power, deeply rooted and strengthened by His love. How much of it are *you* are willing to believe for yourself?

12. Do you see yourself as God's masterpiece? What helps or hinders this truth from being the reality you see when you look in the mirror?

The instant identity change upon believing in Jesus is followed by a slower restoration process. God wants us to be a part of His restoring work in others. But we can either be a flaw-finder, someone who points out all shortcomings and the work that still must be done, or we can be a step-spotter, someone who encourages and points out progress.

13. Describe your experience with a flaw-finder and a step-spotter. How was the process of restoration in your own life affected by both?

Your Good Works: As women, we have a tendency to compare. We want to know if we measure up and to answer that question we can mistakenly look laterally to others rather than to Christ.

I am a Martha. (See Luke 10:38-42!) I like to do. In the past, my measuring stick was *if I can, then I should.* Last year, I hit a point where that was no longer possible. I had neglected rest for too long and was paying a high price for it. I discovered the wonderful word: no. It freed my from saying yes based solely on obligation, pressure or guilt. My new measuring stick was a question for God, "Is this something You would have me do?"

It's far too easy to get sucked into the game of comparison. We can get so focused on what others are doing that we forget we are not called to do what they are called to do. You are called to do what God has called *you* to do. You are responsible to obey what He asks of you.

14. Are you tempted to compare good works with others? Why? If you feel overloaded, what is pressuring you to say yes to too much?

I hear so many women say, *I'm so exhausted, stressed, or too busy*. God-, the author of life, creator of the 24-hour day, and the Sabbath does not desire for you to be exhausted, stressed and overly busy. In John 10:10 Jesus said, *I've come so you may have life to the full.*

There are no exceptions to who He wants abundant life for. He doesn't require any of us to be overextended in order to accomplish His kingdom agenda. He doesn't need anyone to take one for the team. The good works He's planned for you should contribute to abundant life, not take away from it.

What has He asked of you? Encourage a friend? Pray continually? Believe Him? Write? Use your words for building up? Speak the truth in love? Work like He's your only audience? If you have a family is he asking you to respect your husband? Prioritize your family? Train up your children?

15. What good works do you sense He's prepared for you in this present season? What might you need to say no to so you can give God your best yes?

If you're unsure, spend some time asking God. Learn to listen for His voice. You do not need to create a good works proposal. You need only walk in what He's already prepared. I'm certain when you stand before God, He will not ask if you did what *she* did. He might ask, did you do what I asked *you* to do? That is a question we all want to say yes to. Then He will say, *"Well done good and faithful servant. You have been faithful over a little; I will set you over much. Enter into the joy of your master."* (Matt. 25:21, ESV.)

PART 4: BRINGING ME BACK HOME

READ IT: EPHESIANS 2:11-22

[11] Therefore remember that at one time you Gentiles in the flesh, called "the uncircumcision" by what is called the
circumcision, which is made in the flesh by hands— [12] remember that you were at that time separated from Christ,
alienated from the commonwealth of Israel and strangers to the covenants of promise, having no hope and without
God in the world. [13] But now in Christ Jesus you who once were far off have been brought near by the blood of
Christ.14 For he himself is our peace, who has made us both one and has broken down in his flesh the dividing wall
of hostility [15] by abolishing the law of commandments expressed in ordinances, that he might create in himself one
new man in place of the two, so making peace, [16] and might reconcile us both to God in one body through the cross,
thereby killing the hostility. [17] And he came and preached peace to you who were far off and peace to those who
were near. [18] For through him we both have access in one Spirit to the Father. [19] So then you are no longer strangers
and aliens, but you are fellow citizens with the saints and members of the household of God, [20] built on the
foundation of the apostles and prophets, Christ Jesus himself being the cornerstone, [21] in whom the whole structure,
being joined together, grows into a holy temple in the Lord. [22] In him you also are being built together into a dwelling
place for God by the Spirit.

UNPACK IT:

- Underline the words that describe what you once were
- Circle what you now are
- Put a box around how it was made possible, or through whom it was made possible

WORK IT OUT:

Recall the importance of remembering discussed in part 2 (p.22)? God continually commanded His people to remember what He had done for them in the past. Paul calls us to the same action here. When we remember who we were, it points us to who we now are. When we remember areas of our life that were in bondage, it points us to our current state of freedom. We become conscious of the transforming work Jesus Christ has done in our lives.

16. Take a few minutes to remember who you were before meeting Jesus. Think about glimpses of your life with and without the Holy Spirit. Jot down a few specific things He has transformed in your life. Thank Him for all He has rescued you from.

The world we live in offers no real, lasting peace. I recently heard that my generation could suffer from post-traumatic stress disorder from *watching the news*. With each passing day, it seems the world is becoming more dangerous, with an ever-increasing list of things to be concerned about.

God knew how badly and desperately we would need peace. He went to extreme lengths to make it possible for us. Because of His willingness to sacrifice His only son, peace and reconciliation to Him were possible. Because of Jesus, we have been brought near by His blood. The wall of hostility has been broken down. We have full access to Him.

No matter what this life throws our way we have peace with God and we have the peace of God to guard our hearts and our minds in Christ Jesus (Philippians 4:7).

17. In what areas is it challenging for you to let the peace of Christ rule in your heart? (Col. 3:15)

Not only has he brought us back to Him, but He's also made us fellow citizens and members of His household. We are now part of something bigger than ourselves that is being built together.

18. God intends for each of us to connect to a spiritual community; a church family. Where has he called you to serve? In what ways do you sense God is calling you to get involved?

"May the Lord of peace Himself give you peace in every way. The Lord be with all of you. (2 Thess. 3:16, HCSB)

WRAP IT UP:

A phrase I often hear from the mouths of my two toddlers is, "*I do it myself!*" As adults we may not shout it out while stomping our feet, but we are that different. We often think, "*I've* got this."

In John 15:5, Jesus said, "If a man remains in me and I in Him he will bear much fruit. *Apart from me you can do nothing.*" If God's Word says it, I believe it. But believing it doesn't mean I immediately understand how it works. I've always wondered what is the *nothing* Jesus is referring to?

This truth has taken me years to work out because honestly, there are plenty of things I feel fully capable of doing. I also see many who don't know Christ accomplishing a lot more than nothing. This mental wrestling match I was having recently ended when God spoke through one of my favorite teachers: You can do nothing *you can't already do.*

Sure there are some things we can accomplish in our own strength and ability. But do we only want to attempt what we can do in our own strength?

In the last few years, God has taught me the most about His love, His grace and His mercy as I've gotten out of my own boat (see Matthew 14:25-31) and been in situations and relationships that were beyond my ability. There are people I have walked with that I did not have the wisdom to walk with. There are tasks I could not have balanced or accomplished (like writing this Bible study) on my own. Through all of these situations, He has brought me to the same conclusion: *I can't do this on my own.* That realization is what drives us to our knees and has the potential to be the beginning of a new season of growth.

I believe that's where He always wants me to me. I believe that is where His glory is best displayed. God wants us to fully rely on Him because He's got this.

His great love has great purpose for your life. He wants to walk in the good works He has planned for you. And, He loved you enough to sacrifice His Son. He wanted you back with Him, where you belong. Only in His gentle hands can you be restored to the amazing masterpiece He originally intended.

Remember, walking in love flows as you continually understand how you are loved with His great love!

SUMMARIZE what you have learned regarding how He has loved you:

LIVE UP:

Lord, thank you that You didn't leave me where I was, spiritually dead and completely separated from You. Thank you that choosing me had little to do with me and everything to do with Your great love, grace and mercy. Thank you that You have made me alive with Christ and that You have given me the same position as your Son. Thank you for Your grace that saves me from my sin and Your mercy that saves me from all of the consequences of my sin. Do not let me forget that it was a gift. Allow me to remember so that I can share the great news of this free gift with those I encounter. Thank you that I am your masterpiece and when you see me, You see what you originally intended. Continue chiselling away at anything that does not look like You. Help me to discern the good works that You have prepared in advance for me. Help me to say no to what will distract me from Your plans. Thank you that though I was once far off, You have brought me near through Jesus. Thank you so much that I am now at peace with You. Thank you for sending Your Son in order to bring reconciliation in our relationship. Thank you that I now have access to You as a confident child. Thank you that I am now a fellow citizen in Your household. Show me where and how I can be joined together with the rest of Your body so I can continue growing into who You have made me to be. In the powerful name of Jesus, amen.

---

[v] Blueletterbible.org, "Paraptoma," Strong's 3900
[vi] Blueletterbible.org, "Hamartia," Strong's 266
[vii] How People Grow, John Townsend & Henry Cloud, p.265
[viii] Strong's 5485 *Charis,* from the Hebrew Greek Key Study Bible, Word Studies Lexicon to the New Testament;
[ix] Strong's 1656 *Eleos,* from the Hebrew Greek Key Study Bible, Word Studies Lexicon to the New Testament;

WEEK 3: THE GOSPEL

PART 1: GOSPEL MINISTERS

READ IT: EPHESIANS 3:1-6

For this reason I, Paul, a prisoner for Christ Jesus on behalf of you Gentiles—[2] assuming that you have heard of the
stewardship of God's grace that was given to me for you, [3] how the mystery was made known to me by revelation,
as I have written briefly. [4] When you read this, you can perceive my insight into the mystery of Christ, [5] which was
not made known to the sons of men in other generations as it has now been revealed to his holy apostles and
prophets by the Spirit. [6] This mystery is that the Gentiles are fellow heirs, members of the same body, and partakers
of the promise in Christ Jesus through the gospel.

UNPACK IT:

- Where was Paul when he was writing to the Ephesians and why was he there? (v.1)
- Read Acts 20:36-38. Before Paul was put under house arrest in Rome for telling people about Jesus, he spent 3 years in the city of Ephesus teaching and encouraging the new believers. Describe the scene when Paul said good-bye and left the city.
- Underline the word mystery In verses 1-6
- Who was the mystery not made known to? (v.5)
- Underline the 3 things that happen through the gospel. What is the mystery? (v.6)
- Gentiles are non-Jews. If you are not Jewish you are a Gentile. Acts 9:15. At Paul's conversion to Christ what was God's call on his life? The good news through Jesus is that Jews and Gentiles would receive salvation and be one in Christ.

WORK IT OUT:

After my husband Jesse was diagnosed with ALS, we (he and Kathy) were blessed to have many wonderful caregivers in our home. For the first six months, he could still speak. When I came home one day, Susie, his caregiver told me my husband shared the gospel with her and she invited Jesus to come into her life. She was so excited. The gospel is good news. As the disease progressed, we needed more help. When a second caregiver, Nilda, was hired my husband could no longer speak. When Susie was introducing herself to Nilda she said, "I'm thankful I work here because Jesse shared the good news with me when he could still talk and I accepted Jesus. He changed my life." Susie was a brand new Christian but she was already sharing the gospel. On Nilda's second day of work, because of the witness of Susie, she said yes to Jesus.

A few months later, Nilda's mother had a stroke. She travelled back to Europe to be with her family. One sister, Mira, was estranged from the rest of the family. She had not had contact with any of her 7 siblings for more than 8 years. She refused to come to the hospital. Nilda went to her house and knocked repeatedly but Mira would not open the door. Finally, Nilda yelled through the door, "If you don't want to come to the hospital and see our mother before she dies, at least open the door so I can tell you about Jesus before I go back to Canada."

Miraculously, Mira opened the door. Nilda shared the gospel and introduced her sister to Jesus. Nilda received grace and she became a minister of grace. The next day when the family arrived at the hospital, the estranged sister was in the room combing her very weak mother's hair. The family could hardly believe Mira was there. Their brother said, "This is a miracle. If Jesus can change you, I need him too."

Jesus transforms people. He can bring unity and reconciliation. Through Jesus people who are hostile to one another can experience life-changing peace. At that moment they become ministers of the gospel and ministers of grace.

What a joy to watch Jesus work in the lives of these ladies! God transforms lives. Whether we are brand new Christians or if we have known Him for some time, it's our responsibility to tell others. God's plan to take his message of reconciliation to the world is through us. We are ministers of the gospel.

1. Look back at Ephesians 2:14-15 and fill in this truth: Jesus made ____________ and destroyed the wall of ______________. In the Old Testament, God gave a sneak preview of what was to come. Read Isaiah 49:6b and fill in the blank: I will also make you a light to the ________ that you may bring my salvation to __________________________. What does this mean to you?

2. Where does the unifying gospel challenge you? Race? Class distinctions? Poor? Rich? Enemies?

3. How does the gospel help people live in harmony?

4. Are there any relationships in your life that need reconciliation? What does Matthew 5:44 look like in your life? Ask God for help.

5. Where is God calling you to be an ambassador for Him?

PART 2: GRACE TO SHARE

READ IT: EPHESIANS 3:7-13

7 Of this gospel I was made a minister according to the gift of God's grace, which was given me by the working of his
power. 8 To me, though I am the very least of all the saints, this grace was given, to preach to the Gentiles the
unsearchable riches of Christ, 9 and to bring to light for everyone what is the plan of the mystery hidden for ages
in[m] God who created all things, 10 so that through the church the manifold wisdom of God might now be made
known to the rulers and authorities in the heavenly places. 11 This was according to the eternal purpose that he has
realized in Christ Jesus our Lord, 12 in whom we have boldness and access with confidence through our faith in
him. 13 So I ask you not to lose heart over what I am suffering for you, which is your glory.

UNPACK IT:

- What did Paul become a servant of? (v.7)
- When did you become a servant of the gospel?
- Why was God's grace given to Paul? (v.8)
- How can you approach God? (v.12)

WORK IT OUT:

As a young, early twenties woman my life looked good on the outside. I (Kathy) had a great husband, two sweet little girls, a house, two cars and more. This was everything I had dreamed of. So why was I miserable? I struggled with shame over many poor choices I had made. My identity was wrapped up in guilt. I was filled with fear believing people would withdraw love from me if they really knew me. I did not know of God's unconditional love until someone shared the gospel with me. It was good news but I didn't run to Jesus. I took the "long and winding road". Eventually I believed Jesus loved me and died for me. Through Him I received forgiveness when I confessed my sin. He forgave me. I had a new beginning. At that moment I became a servant of the gospel. Just think, I did nothing to deserve it, but God gave me this special joy of serving Him by telling others the good news.

Have you received the gospel? If you received the gospel you are a minister of the gospel. If you received grace you are a minister of grace. Like Paul, you also serve the gospel by sharing it. You became responsible to share the gospel at the moment of your salvation.

6. Read Matthew 4:19. If you follow Jesus what will happen? What does that mean to you?

7. Paul explains that God gave him the responsibility of serving the church by sharing the gospel. Write out Colossians 1:25. What are your thoughts about God giving you the assignment of sharing the gospel?

8. In verse 8, Paul describes himself as the least. Without God's help or God's power Paul would not be able to do God's work. Identify ways God has continued to rescue you since your initial point of salvation. Into what areas has He infused life?

9. Your greatest struggles can become your most powerful ministries. Describe any opportunities He has given you to minister to others in these areas.

10. Do you view ministering to people as pouring yourself out, or a way that God also pours in to you? Explain.

11. When an opportunity presents itself to share the gospel do you feel prepared? How could you get ready?

12. God wants to use you to share the gospel. Write out 1 Peter 3:15. Write down the names of 4 people in your circle of influence who do not know Jesus. Ask God to give you an opportunity to share the gospel with them.

The first change I saw in my life after I trusted Christ was a desire to read the Bible, a book I had never opened. Thankfully that was an inside change God made in my life. Although I love to read and study the word of God, I don't find it as easy to spend extended time in prayer. If I'm studying the Bible I can spend hours but I can't seem to pray for very long. A few years ago, I wanted to have more intentional time in prayer. I decided to pray for 30 minutes and put the timer on. In the middle of my prayer time I found myself in the basement folding laundry. What happened? While praying, I remembered the load of laundry that was in the dryer and without thinking I got up, walked downstairs and started folding. When I came to my senses and realized I was distracted, what did I do? I quit folding the laundry and went back to praying. I reconnected. I'm still working at strengthening my connection. I'm doing a little more praying and a little less folding during my connecting time.

13. What distracts you from connecting to Jesus on a day-to-day basis? How can you strengthen your connection?

PART 3: BEING THE GOSPEL

READ IT: EPHESIANS 2:10

[14] For this reason I bow my knees before the Father, [15] from whom every family in heaven and on earth is
named, [16] that according to the riches of his glory he may grant you to be strengthened with power through his
Spirit in your inner being, [17] so that Christ may dwell in your hearts through faith—that you, being rooted
and grounded in love, [18] may have strength to comprehend with all the saints what is the breadth and length
and height and depth, [19] and to know the love of Christ that surpasses knowledge, that you may be filled with all the
fullness of God.

[20] Now to him who is able to do far more abundantly than all that we ask or think, according to the power at work
within us, [21] to him be glory in the church and in Christ Jesus throughout all generations, forever and ever. Amen.

UNPACK IT:

Paul has just written that we have boldness and confidence through our faith in Jesus. He opens his prayer with "for *this* reason." He's about to boldly and confidently ask for something critically important to the Christian life.

- Circle the action words that Paul is asking for on our behalf. (v.16-10)
- Underline the following: Where does the strengthening take place? How are we strengthened? How does Christ dwell in our hearts? What kind of knowledge of His love are we to have?
- What is the result of knowing the love of Christ that surpasses knowledge? (v.19)
- Underline the description of what God is able to do. (v.20)

WORK IT OUT:

What Paul asks for here is the opposite of what the world expects. The world tells us to pull ourselves together on the outside. It's too easy to prioritize getting together outward things and think that our strength for life will come from reaching a certain marker in our finances, relationships, careers or pursuits. It's easy to believe that once our external circumstances change, then we will be better positioned to put God first, serve Him or spend time in His Word.

I better understood the meaning of the word dwell (from "katoikeo") when I looked at the opposite description. The opposite of dwell is: to be a stranger, sojourner, temporary, not settled, for a time...

Jesus doesn't want merely to make appearances in our lives. He's not so busy that He can only pass through when we have an urgent need. He wants to set up shop permanently.

True change happens from the inside out. Paul asks that we are strengthened in our inner being. The real solution isn't to pursue strength from worldly endeavors but to allow Christ to make our heart His home.

1. Read Matthew 6:33. What are we to seek first? What is the promised result?

There are pieces of knowledge that we possess in our heads, and then there are realities we have experienced in our hearts. This prayer of Paul's is one I have read through and prayed through many times in my life. A couple of years ago I had the opportunity to share at my church ladies retreat a message about God's love that He had made so real in my life. The following day, I was reading through this passage and every word resonated deep within my Spirit in such a real and tangible way. I thought, this is what He is talking about! I get it.

We do not need those experiences in order for truth to stand in our lives, but when God brings something to life like that, there's nothing quite like it. That weekend, I experienced a very real glimpse of the fullness of God as a result of being rooted and grounded in His love.

I love the picture given here. Picture an oak tree that is deeply rooted and grounded. It's almost immovable. It draws it's nutrients from the soil it's planted in. It is strong; it can withstand storms and can be a shelter. It's no flimsy thing. Being able to comprehend God's great love requires strength and being established in the truth of God's love. Though we can feel sprinkled with it here and there at different points in our lives, God's desire is that His love is deeply ingrained in us. It is to be the soil we draw strength from and the thing that enables us to continue walking steadily.

2. Based on Ephesians 3:16-19, what did Paul believe was central to the Christian life? How does this differ from what we often believe to be the primary purpose of the Christian life?

3. Which better reflects your attitude towards loving others: I love because He first loved me? Or I love because I'm supposed to love?

4. Read and meditate (prayerfully think) on verse 20-21. In your life what could God want to do that would be beyond your wildest dreams? What would you be freed from? What would occupy your thoughts? What story would your life tell?

WRAP IT UP:

We need to be gospel people. We must give attention to the gospel, be defined by gospel and solve our problems by applying the gospel.[x]

This week, I hope God has stirred in you a desire for the gospel. Our human nature will always lean toward independence. In this case, the default may be *I will try harder to be a minister of the gospel.*

Instead, of turning to performance, turn to connection. *Lord, take me deeper into the gospel. You want this to be the overflow of my life, but it cannot be until it goes down deep and changes who I am. Help me not to see the gospel as only the starting point of our relationship, but the thing that continually shapes my life. As you are doing that, give me opportunities to minister the grace that you are ministering to me. Make me the cherry tree.* The deeper you are rooted in His love, the more the gospel will flow from your life.

Confidence comes from conviction. The biggest problem in bringing the boldness offered in this passage into our lives is that often we are not convinced of the truth of our own gospel.

I believe the truth of our own gospel is recognizing how the gospel continually works in day to day life. The gospel is *Jesus in my place*. He died, was buried and rose again on the third day. Through a personal struggle, God has begun to show me the truth of the gospel at work in my life in an ongoing way. (I chose general terms because I want you to think about how this might work in your own struggle.)

I have struggled with this certain something for as long as I can remember. I failed to recognize it as a spiritual struggle because it's not a habit listed in the New Testament right next to the command to *"put to death"* or *"those who _______ will not inherit the kingdom of God."* It is what we might call a "socially acceptable" sin (as if there were such a thing) as it's not overtly destructive in nature. It also blends well into my personality which made it a little trickier to uncover.

In my mind, my lack of victory in this area of my life was simply a result of lack of effort. It was something I had always asked for God's help with but long-lasting victory continued to elude me. My try-harder solution came up short every time. I could relate to Paul: *the thing I want to do I cannot do and the very thing I hate, this is what I do.* It wasn't until a few months ago that I began to think, maybe there's more to this. How many years does one have to pray the same prayer and experience the same failure before realizing it isn't something that can be fixed by mere human effort?

Around the same time I was at a training conference when the leader said, "*Maybe your thing is* (what my thing was). *We all know what that is rooted in, right?* (I was all ears.) *Fear of failure. You might still think you can overcome it just by trying harder. You're wrong."*

I sat there feeling slightly naked. *How* did he know? My losing battle had flown under the radar as "not so bad," "just who I am," "part of my personality" and something I'll one day get a grip on. But God was confirming what I was beginning to suspect was true-- there was more to it.

As I read through Ephesians 2:1-10 and reflected on the truth of the gospel a pattern emerged. Perhaps even a gospel pattern that can be applied to change in our lives. We commonly think of Ephesians 2 as applying only to our initial moment of salvation.

Salvation is three part: justification (our identity change), sanctification (process of becoming like Jesus) and glorification (heaven anyone?). Perhaps then, this truth can continually apply to our ongoing sanctification. Instead of thinking I can overcome ______ in my life by trying harder, maybe I ought to think this way:

- **You were dead.** I have exhausted my efforts and come to a point of realization that this is not something I can overcome merely by trying harder or increasing my effort. This part of me is dead, unable to resurrect itself or come to life.
- **But God.** Hallelujah. He didn't leave me in my overall state of spiritual deadness and He certainly doesn't want to leave any part of the flesh that is causing death untouched so it can continue to wreak havoc in my life.
- **Made us alive.** He's the only one who can do this. Why? Remember Jesus? He was dead, in the literal sense. Heart stopped. No pulse. Not breathing. Not moving. Not just asleep... DEAD. Separated from God. God proved that He could resurrect the dead. Can you think of anything in this world harder to overcome than that? I certainly can't.
- **Raised us up.** He gave us the same position as Christ (seated us next to Him in heavenly places) which means He has given us victory. Repeat after me: He has given me ***VICTORY*** in Jesus. If you shouted a little that's okay too.
- **That he might show the riches of His grace in kindness towards us.** This phrase should be getting familiar by now. Our lives put Him on display. The more areas of deadness we have, the more areas of our lives He can bring to life and bring victory, the more the world gets to see the riches of His grace and kindness.
- **By grace you have been saved through faith.** Will you recognize the gift here? What He is rescuing you from is a gift and comes as you respond to Him in faith.
- **This is not your own doing. Not a result of works.** This is easily forgotten in our world that celebrates high achievers. With God, the way up is down. If you want victory, you want Him to work, you want to see Him show up, you need to stop thinking, I have got this. If I only try a little harder, organize myself a bit better. It was not a result of my own works but of God's great mercy and grace.
- **We are his workmanship, created for good works.** His ongoing work in my life continues to show the world the great Artist that He is and often will point me in the direction of the good works He has in store.

Perhaps this is truly the way to see victory in our lives. Not by depending on our own abilities, but recognizing the spiritual deadness of our problems, big or small. We need enlightenment to see the areas of our lives that are lacking the abundance available to us. We need to solve life's problems by continually applying the gospel, rather than thinking, I have got it from here.

5. What are you currently struggling with that you cannot overcome by your own effort? How does the gospel apply in your life today?

SUMMARIZE what you have learned regarding the gospel and your role:

LIVE UP:

Lord, You made this all possible by sending Jesus Christ to die for me. Continue showing me how this impacts my day to day living. Thank you that You have made me a fellow heir and that I get to partake in the promises of Christ Jesus because of the gospel. Thank you for making me a steward of grace by Your great power. Show me how my words and actions can bring to light Your wisdom. Thank you that I have boldness and confident access to You through faith. Strengthen me with Your power in my inner being. I want Christ to be at home in my heart. Increase my faith so this is possible. Ground me and root my deeply in Your love. No matter how much of Your love I have experienced, there is always more. May I know Your love in a way that surpasses knowledge. Make it my experience so I may be filled with all the fullness You have to offer. You are able to do so much more than I can even fathom. Increase my faith to believe that You will do powerful things in and through my life. Let me never forget it's all for Your glory, not my own. In the powerful name of Jesus, amen.

---

[x] Gospel Revolution, J.D. Greear,

WEEK 4: BEHAVIOUR THAT FOLLOWS BELIEF

DONE, THEREFORE DO

It's far too tempting to look at this passage independently of the three previous chapters and slip into the independent woman mentality. But we are called to live in a way that reflects an understanding of all He has given us and all He has done on our behalf.

I recently saw am impactful dramatic representation of the story of the prodigal son, only it was a prodigal daughter. She was adopted into the family but never embraced her identity as a daughter. The father made many attempts at strengthening their relationship. He wanted to be with her. All she knew how to do was strive. She was constantly trying to please him by working in ways that she thought he required, rather than accepting that He was pleased simply because she was his. She eventually became resentful of all her own efforts, mistakenly thinking it was required by her father despite the fact that He never required any of it. It reminded me of this quote:

"Gospel-centered change is not about giving you a list of things you need to go and do for God, but making you stand in awe of what He has done for you."[xi]

It's a subtle difference that is hardly detectable from the outside looking in. When I change my behaviour before my heart, I'm seeking something from God. I'm seeking His approval rather than realizing I already have it through Jesus Christ just like the prodigal daughter. It matters that we seek inside-out change. A transformed heart is the difference between religious duty and a life overflowing from being filled.

It's easy to read Ephesians 4-6 and think only of what we need to do for God. We cannot forget to stand in awe of what He has done for us. A great reminder can always be found in Ephesians 1-3.

This week, you will continue to see how walking in love is a reflection of a loving relationship. A growing relationship with Him ignites a desire to live in a manner worthy of the invitation to salvation and spiritual blessings. This is the calling we have all received.

I believe God also gives us each a specific calling or purposeful part in the body. Our specific calling is the intersection of our giftedness and burden.[xii] There are endless opportunities to serve. But I believe it is our burden that directs us to where our gifts can be most effectively used. Our burden Is often shaped by what we have experienced of God because we desperately desire others with similar struggles to know and believe the same about Him. We often experience Him as we are sanctified through His Word, circumstances, the Holy Spirit and relationships. All of this takes place as we walk in relationship with Him.

I'm praying for you as you get into the Word this week!

PART 1: A WORTHY WALK

READ IT: EPHESIANS 4:1-6

I therefore, a prisoner for the Lord, urge you to walk in a manner worthy of the calling to which you have been
called, 2 with all humility and gentleness, with patience, bearing with one another in love, 3 eager to maintain the
unity of the Spirit in the bond of peace. 4 There is one body and one Spirit—just as you were called to the one hope
that belongs to your call— 5 one Lord, one faith, one baptism, 6 one God and Father of all, who is over all and
through all and in all.

UNPACK IT:

- Circle the word that describes the tone of Paul's appeal to believers
- Underline the describing words that characterize a life worthy of the call (v.2-3)
- What are we maintaining? (v.3) Why are we maintaining it? (v.4-5)

WORK IT OUT:

Is your life characterized by what Paul is describing? I believe that these qualities reflect an understanding of what we have received in Christ. Walking in a worthy manner of the calling we have received is only possible when we have actually *received* what has been given to us. As we continually receive what He has made available to us, this response will continually flow out of us.

Humility means having a humble opinion on one's self or an awareness that all we have is from God. It means, *"arriving at a correct estimation of ourselves resulting from emptying of ourselves. Those with authentic humility are those who practice aggressive confession, thus developing a deep unworthiness to receive God's marvelous grace."*[xiii]

1. Did your study of Ephesians 1-3 help you arrive at a more correct estimation of yourself? How might this would this result in humility?

Gentleness is defined as "not an expression of feeling but inward grace of the soul first and foremost towards God where we accept His dealings with us as good without resisting or disputing."[xiv] Life's challenges can make this difficult to live out because not everything God permits in our lives feels pleasant. There is much we want to resist and dispute. Pain that we experience can make it tempting to forget that God is rich in mercy and grace toward us.

2. What challenges in your life have made it difficult to display gentleness— accepting God's dealings with you as good? Do you measure His compassion by the cross, or have life's difficulties made it challenging for you to recall that He is merciful and gracious toward you?

The patience that Paul is describing here is from the word *makrothumia* which specifies patience with respect to people. (Patience with circumstances is often translated *endurance*.) Patience is inspired by mercy and literally means to hold back or show self-restraint before proceeding to action.

3. In light of Ephesians 2:1-9, why would a life worthy of the call reflect patience? What does your current level of patience or mercy with people reflect about your understanding of God's mercy and patience with you?

Next, Paul says we are to bear with one another in love. Other translations say "*accepting one another in love* (HCSB)", "*showing tolerance for one another in love*" (NASB) or "*making allowances for each other's faults because of your love*" (NLT). It's easy to fear the words tolerance or acceptance in our culture because accepting or tolerating people can be confused with accepting or tolerating sin.

4. Read Romans 15:1-13. Write out verse seven in the space below. According to verse nine, what will accepting others ultimately cause others to do, and for what?

When we pause long enough to remember the state we were in when God saved us, and the way that He continues to love us in spite of our struggles, the motivation for accepting others is clear: *"As Christ accepted you."* Acceptance creates an atmosphere for change. Withholding acceptance in hopes of motivating people to change creates an atmosphere of judgment.

We are to be eager to maintain peace. Unity is so close to the heart of Jesus that He prayed earnestly for it among the disciples before He left earth (John 17:20-23). The enemy is always looking to divide and conquer, especially among those in the body of Christ (1 Peter 5:8, John 10:10).

5. What does Paul list as the reason to maintain the bond of peace? How can living with this reality simplify the lines we sometimes choose to divide on?

In Christ, we are one body, empowered by one Spirit, under one God who is over all. The Creator of creativity Himself left plenty of room for there to be differences within His kingdom. However, matters of preference should not take priority over peace and unity.

6. What issues are you tempted to prioritize over protecting the peace that Jesus Christ paid for?

A walk characterized by humility, gentleness, patience, forbearance and peace is a walk worthy of the calling we have received because it reflects that we have received. It is evidence that we are continually being affected by a present tense loving relationship with Jesus Christ.

PART 2: A PURPOSEFUL PART

READ IT: EPHESIANS 4:7-16

7 But grace was given to each one of us according to the measure of Christ's gift. 8 Therefore it says, "When he
ascended on high he led a host of captives, and he gave gifts to men." 9 (In saying, "He ascended," what does it
mean but that he had also descended into the lower regions, the earth? 10 He who descended is the one who also
ascended far above all the heavens, that he might fill all things.) 11 And he gave the apostles, the prophets,
the evangelists, the shepherds and teachers, 12 to equip the saints for the work of ministry, for building up the body
of Christ, 13 until we all attain to the unity of the faith and of the knowledge of the Son of God, to mature
manhood, to the measure of the stature of the fullness of Christ, 14 so that we may no longer be children, tossed to
and fro by the waves and carried about by every wind of doctrine, by human cunning, by craftiness in deceitful
schemes. 15 Rather, speaking the truth in love, we are to grow up in every way into him who is the head, into
Christ, 16 from whom the whole body, joined and held together by every joint with which it is equipped, when each
part is working properly, makes the body grow so that it builds itself up in love.

UNPACK IT:

- What was given according to the measure of Christ's gift and to whom was it given? (v.7)
- Underline the two purposes of God giving gifts to men in v.12.
- What are the goals of these two purposes? (v.13-16)
- How do we grow up in every way according to v.15?
- What is the end result of the body being joined, held together, and working properly? (v.16)

WORK IT OUT:

God has given every one of us a specific measure of grace for ministry. Intimidation can easily accompany the word ministry but it simply means service, helping someone or caring for a need. Any type of work that benefits others is a *diakonia* (the word translated ministry or service.) I've often heard phrases like, "All I can do is..." or "I *just...*" The significance of meeting needs can be easily overlooked if we don't identify as an apostle, evangelist, prophet, shepherd or teacher but it shouldn't be.

I received a beautifully written card of encouragement from a friend the Father's day after my dad had passed on. I received meals after having a baby. I've received words of affirmation as I've pursued what I feel God has called me to do. I've received emails saying that I've been remembered in prayer. I have friends who have watched my kids so I could have time to write or rest.

Each time I've been a recipient of grace from another person, I have been built up or encouraged in some way. I've been reminded of God's love, provision and care for me. I am so incredibly thankful for those who respond in obedience to whatever God asks of them. The body benefits when we obey.

7. What needs has God enabled you to meet? Do you value the grace God has given you for the building up of the body?

8. Calling can be understood as an intersection between your giftedness and your burden.[xv] Who or what do you feel burdened for? What gifts has God given you? Where do your giftedness and burden meet?

The goal of us all walking in the calling we have received is for the body to be built up. We are to promote growth in one another. He wants our knowledge of Him to be correct and experiential, not just theoretical. He desires that we become mature and experience the fullness of Christ.

To be mature in Christ means to be complete or fully grown. The one who is mature is one who is obedient in Christ. But it doesn't mean one that is perfectly sinless. This concept of maturity is not a static state, meaning we reach it and remain there. We don't get to graduate to being a mature Christian with honours and then hang our degree on the wall. The more obedient we are in our relationship with God, the more ways Christ will continue to be formed in us.

9. When you look back, what are some areas of your life that God has matured in you? Who or what did He use in that process? Ask Him to show you where you can be a similar instrument in the life of another.

One of the ways this maturing process takes place is when we speak the truth in love and when the truth is spoken to us in love. Truth is necessary for growth and for the proper working of each part of the body. Speaking the truth includes correction and encouragement.

I was recently doing an exercise where I had to list personal character defects and flaws. As you can imagine, it was thrilling. I asked a good friend for her input on my lengthy list. While she lovingly agreed with the entire list, she also pointed out how many of the flaws also had the potential to be used of God if not misunderstood or misused. I left the conversation feeling encouraged rather than in despair.

I realized that truth does not always need be housed in a hammer. It's easy to think of speaking the truth exclusively as correction and rebuke. We must remember that speaking the truth includes speaking life. It leaves people feeling in tact even when they are being corrected.

10. Ask God who in your life needs to hear truth in love. What might He have you say on His behalf?

Remember, there are no unspiritual acts of service. The criteria for service is that it meets the need of a person and builds up the body. If you belong to Him, He has given you grace to share among the body He has placed you in. The body needs you and you need the body so that each part can work properly!

PART 3: MORE LIKE HIM

READ IT: EPHESIANS 4:17-32

[17] Now this I say and testify in the Lord, that you must no longer walk as the Gentiles do, in the futility of their
minds. [18] They are darkened in their understanding, alienated from the life of God because of the ignorance that is in
them, due to their hardness of heart. [19] They have become callous and have given themselves up to sensuality,
greedy to practice every kind of impurity.[20] But that is not the way you learned Christ!— [21] assuming that you have
heard about him and were taught in him, as the truth is in Jesus, [22] to put off your old self, which belongs to your
former manner of life and is corrupt through deceitful desires, [23] and to be renewed in the spirit of your
minds, [24] and to put on the new self, created after the likeness of God in true righteousness and
holiness.[25] Therefore, having put away falsehood, let each one of you speak the truth with his neighbor, for we are
members one of another. [26] Be angry and do not sin; do not let the sun go down on your anger, [27] and give no
opportunity to the devil. [28] Let the thief no longer steal, but rather let him labor, doing honest work with his own
hands, so that he may have something to share with anyone in need. [29] Let no corrupting talk come out of your
mouths, but only such as is good for building up, as fits the occasion, that it may give grace to those who
hear. [30] And do not grieve the Holy Spirit of God, by whom you were sealed for the day of redemption. [31] Let all
bitterness and wrath and anger and clamor and slander be put away from you, along with all malice. [32] Be kind to
one another, tender hearted, forgiving one another, as God in Christ forgave you.

UNPACK IT:

- Underline what characterizes as the futility of mind. (v.18-19)
- What two things does Paul assume about those who have learned Christ? (v.21)
- Put a box around what we have been taught to do in Christ. (v.22-24)
- Underline what we are told to put off and circle what we are instructed to put on instead. (v.25-31)
- What is the motivation for being kind, tender-hearted and forgiving toward one another? (v.32)

WORK IT OUT:

I love makeover style shows because of the dramatic change that takes place. On *What Not to Wear,* video footage is collected of the contestant's fashion faux paus. They are later surprised by experts on all the fashion crimes they are committing. Before they can receive the makeover of a lifetime, they must surrender control of their existing wardrobe to the experts to determine if it is trash or worth keeping. There is usually some resistance during this sifting process, but once they give up control they receive a loaded VISA to purchase a new wardrobe according to the new guidelines. At the end of 60 minutes, there is a brand new person with little recognizable trace of the old.

This last section of Ephesians 4 reads a little like this plot line. We are given a contrast between old and new. Before we can put on the new, the old has to go. There isn't room for both. They cannot compete.

I was once asked by a new believer if we ever graduate from Sunday school. It was a fair question as every other school in this world does have a finish line! I told her our finish line is heaven because we are always learning and growing.

As we live in relationship with God, we are continually sanctified. We never graduate from this process. We never reach a point of maturity on this earth where we no longer need to continue the pattern and process of putting off the old self, renewing the mind, and putting on the new self. In Psalm 139:23-24, David asks God to search His heart to see if there is any offensive way in Him. He recognizes that God knows the depths of his heart in ways he does not.

In my experience, God always reveals something that needs to go. Sometimes the things that need to go are the habits, patterns of thinking, and ways of living that have been put off before but have crept back in. We must ask and then listen intently with expectation that He will answer. Sometimes He responds immediately and others times He answers over time.

11. Read Psalm 139:23-24. Ask God to examine your heart and see if there is any offensive way in you. Has God revealed any of the old in your life that needs to go? How have you responded?

In case we don't have eyes to see where the old has continued to dwell in our hearts and minds, Paul spends a few verses giving specifics. The old self is characterized by spiritual blindness which results in the futility of the mind (meaning devoid of truth and appropriateness), being darkened in understanding and alienated from the life of God. Without God's objective truth as our measuring stick, our minds are easily pulled towards futility.

What amuses me on What Not to Wear is how badly people want to hang on to their old wardrobes. I cannot help but think and perhaps shout, Why?! It really truly looks *awful*. Do you not realize you get a whole new and much better wardrobe? I'm sure Paul felt the same way. The things that we often cling to don't flatter us nor do they fit with our identity in Christ.

Our world today has no shortage of ways to full our minds with things that are eternally useless, worthless or empty. This is not to be confused with rest or enjoying what God has given us. On the contrary, rest is commanded by God, productive and necessary.

12. Are you tempted to fill your mind with futile things? Are there any futile things you can remove from your life this week to make room for more of God's best?

We are then reminded that that is *not* the way you learned Christ with a little caveat that cannot be overlooked: assuming you have heard *and have been taught in Him* as the truth is in Jesus.

Our world is much more populated with converts and church goers than those who have been taught in the truth. It's fairly easy to recognize behaviors or a lifestyle that is not consistent with God's truth. While it is tempting to point others to mere mechanical change, perhaps the bigger problem is a life that has not heard or been taught in the truth.

13. Knowing and understanding the truth manifests itself in a changed life. What areas of your life reflect that you need to hear more of Christ and be taught in His truth?

In this case we have trouble identifying traces of the old, Paul clearly tells us that falsehood, anger, stealing, corrupt talk, bitterness, rage, anger, brawling and slander have absolutely no place in our new life with Christ. Those things need to be trashed much like the awful wardrobe.

Social media allows people to display only the parts of their lives they want others to see. People can skim the highlight reel and believe that

picture perfect life must be free of challenge and conflict.

14. Falsehood is *anything different from what it professes to be*. Besides outright lying, it can include exaggeration, denial, hyper-focusing on negatives, omission, or lack of authenticity. Is there any falsehood in your life that needs to be put off?

Speaking the truth with your neighbor does not mean airing detailed dirty laundry to every person you encounter. I recently heard a brilliant challenge: *Authenticity with all. Transparency with most. Intimacy with some.*[xvi] I believe the difference between the three levels of truthfulness lies in the details. We can be authentic without being overly specific. The details should not distract from God's work.

15. Think of a specific struggle you have had or are having. What would authenticity with all look or sound like? What would transparency with most look or sound like? What would intimacy with some look or sound like?

We are permitted to be angry but are warned to not allow it to lead to sin or to allow it to be a long-term guest in our hearts. Harbouring anger can give the enemy a foothold in our lives. Anger is often rooted in the belief that there is something we are owed. For example, I may become upset with a person when they don't meet an expectation that I had. I may feel they owed it to me to live up to it.

16. Think of the last time you became angry. What did you feel owed and who did you feel owed it to you?

    Is there unresolved anger in your life you have allowed the sun to go down on rather than allowing God to deal with it? If so, ask Him to allow the truth of verse 32 to permeate your anger.

Unwholesome or corrupt talk is anything that is unfit for use. It can be rooted in unforgiveness, bitterness, envy, resentment, carelessness, thoughtlessness, ignorance, pride, self-pity, fear or guilt. If the criteria for our speech was usefulness, we would probably say a lot less. When we are preoccupied with praise, thanksgiving, encouragement, and speaking the truth, there isn't too much time left for unwholesome or corrupt talk.

17. When are you most tempted to allow corrupt talk to come out of your mouth? What two purposes should our words serve?

18. How does continually remembering that we are forgiven by God enable us to be kind, compassionate and forgiving towards others?

19. Are there other things that do not fit with your new identity (bitterness, rage, anger, brawling, or slander) but you are reluctant to let go of? When you think of letting go of the old, what fears surface?

WRAP IT UP: SETTLING INTO THE PROCESS

This past fall I decided it was time to learn how to properly apply makeup. I went to a makeup store where a lovely girl showed me in 15 minutes how to apply perfect foundation, bronzer and blush. I left with some useful products in tow but still needing more instruction. I went and saw an esthetician friend who gave me full application lessons so I would know what to do with my useful products. She applied the left side of my face and allowed me to attempt the right side under her supervision. I left feeling confident I could replicate my new look the next day in approximately 5 minutes. After all, that is how long the experts say your everyday look should take.

The next day I attempted to replicate what I had learned. It took much longer than five minutes. I came downstairs where my loving husband's response was to burst into laughter. I took that as a hint that this application business may take some time to get right. There was more than one morning where my application was immediately followed by washing my face. I quickly realized that my two application lessons didn't guarantee immediate professional results. It would take some time and a lot of working out before my finished product didn't elicit laughter and could pass as natural. It's no wonder that Paul says in Philippians 2:12, "*Continue* to work out your salvation with fear and trembling."

A life worthy of the call cannot be completely understood and put into perfect practice after a week of Bible study. It is worked out over time in relationship with Him in a similar way that a marriage relationship is worked out over years or decades; only He is the perfect lover of our soul! In order to live a life of love we must always remain connected to Love. There is much to be unpacked together and experienced.

This morning I told my hubby, I *will* conquer this makeup business. Now I just know to settle into the process because it's going to take some time.

SUMMARIZE what you have learned regarding living your life worthy of the calling you have received:

LIVE UP:

Lord, give me an understanding of the calling I have received. Give me a heart to respond to it with all humility, gentleness, patience and forbearance motivated by what You already did. Put within me an understanding that all the individual calls on lives are for one purpose. They are not more or less important but different. Give me a desire to maintain the unity and peace that You paid such a high price for. Give me Your eyes to see what You have called me to do. You have given many different gifts but You have wired me in a specific way. Show me where my giftedness and burden intersect. You have called me to be a part of building up the body of Christ. Show me where I can do that and how. Your desire is that together, we would be mature and experience the fullness of Christ. Your desire is not for me to remain a child, and to be tossed to and fro by the waves, but to be strengthened as I grow up in You. I need to be a functioning part of the body in order for it to work properly. Show me where my understanding has been darkened, where I'm blinded by ignorance or where my heart has been hardened. I cannot discern these things on my own. In Your strength, I need to put off my old self. I know there are still parts lingering, but I cannot always recognize them. Renew my mind in Your truth and in Your Spirit so I can put on the new self in righteousness and holiness. Show me where I have not been able to be honest with myself and others. Put truth within my perspective and my heart. Show me where anger resides and how to release it to you when I'm tempted to harbour it. Make me a good steward of what You've entrusted to me so I may have something to share with those in need. Guard my heart and my mouth so only what is useful for building others up comes out and my words minister grace. Remove bitterness, wrath, anger and slander from my heart and replace it with the truth that You have forgiven me because of Your great love. Because of that, through You, I can do the same. In the powerful name of Jesus, Amen.

---

xi Gospel Revolution Workbook, J.D. Greear, p.11
xii Lifeway Women's Devotional CD, Volume 2, "Freefall to Fly, Rebekah Lyons"
xiii The Complete Word Study Dictionary
xiv Vines Expository Dictionary
xv Lifeway Women's Devotional CD, Volume 2, "Freefall to Fly, Rebekah Lyons"
xvi Sacred Secrets, Beth Moore

WEEK 5: IMITATORS

PART 1: ON PURPOSE

READ IT: EPHESIANS 5:1-20

5 Therefore be imitators of God, as beloved children. **2** And walk in love, as Christ loved us and gave himself up for us, a fragrant offering and sacrifice to God. **3** But sexual immorality and all impurity or covetousness must not even be named among you, as is proper among saints. **4** Let there be no filthiness nor foolish talk nor crude joking, which are out of place, but instead let there be thanksgiving. **5** For you may be sure of this, that everyone who is sexually immoral or impure, or who is covetous (that is, an idolater), has no inheritance in the kingdom of Christ and God. **6** Let no one deceive you with empty words, for because of these things the wrath of God comes upon the sons of disobedience. **7** Therefore do not become partners with them; **8** for at one time you were darkness, but now you are light in the Lord. Walk as children of light **9** (for the fruit of light is found in all that is good and right and true), **10** and try to discern what is pleasing to the Lord. **11** Take no part in the unfruitful works of darkness, but instead expose them. **12** For it is shameful even to speak of the things that they do in secret. **13** But when anything is exposed by the light, it becomes visible, **14** for anything that becomes visible is light. Therefore it says, "Awake, O sleeper, and arise from the dead, and Christ will shine on you." **15** Look carefully then how you walk, not as unwise but as wise, **16** making the best use of the time, because the days are evil. **17** Therefore do not be foolish, but understand what the will of the Lord is. **18** And do not get drunk with wine, for that is debauchery, but be filled with the Spirit, **19** addressing one another in psalms and hymns and spiritual songs, singing and making melody to the Lord with your heart, **20** giving thanks always and for everything to God the Father in the name of our Lord Jesus Christ, **21** submitting to one another out of reverence for Christ.

UNPACK IT:

- Who are we to imitate and how? (v.1 2)
- What is to characterize our speech? (v.4)
- What is at stake for those who continue to walk in those areas of darkness? (v.5)
- How are we to walk and what is the fruit of it? (v.8-9)
- What happens when things are exposed to the light? (v.13-14)
- What is wise walking characterized by? (v.15-21)

WORK IT OUT:

As dearly loved children, we are to imitate our Father. My toddlers are little sponges. I often hear them say things or copy both my husband's and my mannerisms. These things haven't been taught to them but they've been learned by being in close relationship with us. This is the secret to walking in love: *as Christ loved us.* Our love should reflect His love because He is our Father. When it doesn't, we may have lost touch with Him. I hope you have experienced a fresh measure of God's love for you as you have been studying. As our understanding of His love grows, we are freed and fueled to love those around us the way God does.

1. It's easier to believe that God so *loved* us and even that God *loves* us. But knowing God is *loving* you seems to be harder to see. Scripture tells us that every good and perfect gift is from above (James 1:17). What gifts has he bestowed on you recently that remind you of His love for you in a present and ongoing way?

2. Christ's love for us ultimately led Him to lay down His life. How would imitating His example look in your life today?

The rhythm of life will always pull us away from God's unchanging standard. This is why we must be intentional about exposing our lives to truth.

As beloved children, gratitude should be the attitude of our lives. If we are constantly aware of what God has given us, how could we not be grateful? It's no wonder that thanksgiving is to characterize our speech because our words are simply the overflow of our hearts (Matthew 12:34).

We can be so aware of God's continual love and grace in our lives that gratitude fills our hearts and spills out of us as we speak. We can also practice the discipline of gratitude. Even when our emotions are not cooperating, we can choose to notice the good things in our lives and give thanks. He is the Giver of all. Whether gratitude is exercised from a place of discipline or delight, it exposes your life to the person who is Truth because you are acknowledging His ongoing provision.

3. Write out 1 Thessalonians 5:18 in the space below. List five things you are thankful for right now.

4. How could thanksgiving so fully take over your speech that foolish talk has no room?

I love springtime. There are signs of new life popping up everywhere largely due to the increasing temperatures and daylight. The light brings new life but also a reality check. One of my least favorite activities is spring cleaning. Once light starts pouring through the windows and the presence of dirt and dust becomes impossible to ignore, cleaning seems like the appropriate response. Light exposes and reveals what the darkness cannot. As necessary as it may be, the idea of deep cleaning the entire house is overwhelming to me. As it is with any intimidating task, it's easy to be a master of avoidance.

5. Are there any areas of your life you're afraid to expose to the light? Why is this?

Thankfully, when it comes to exposing our hearts to the truth, we don't need to figure out how to do the deep clean by ourselves. Through the sealing work of the Holy Spirit (Ephesians 1:13) we are completely secure in our relationship with God. This gives us the safety we need to be completely real. He does the sanctifying. Our job is to seek Him, ask for Him and follow Him.[xvii]

The Holy Spirit's job and our role are tough concepts for our human minds. I've tried to understand it in black and white terms but it cannot be simplified to percentages or job descriptions. We must be actively dependent.

> *"The Spirit-filled life is a supernatural life that surpasses our strength and abilities.... But this does not mean that we do not have to do anything. We still have to step out in faith. We have to risk. We have to love, open up, confess, reach out, repent, obey, and do all the other things we are commanded to do. Our part is to live the life. But we do not have to do it alone or in our power. We are partners with the Spirit."*[xviii]

6. Is your tendency to lean towards being dependent (doing less) or active (doing more) when it comes to spiritual growth? Give one example of what being a *dependently active* partner with the Spirit would look like.

The things that are out of place for children of light (sexual immorality, impurity, covetousness or idolatry, filthiness, foolish talk, and crude joking) are not forbidden just to punish us. They rob you of the joy, safety, satisfaction and reward of a loving relationship with God. In addition, these things of darkness occupy valuable space in our hearts, minds and time that push out the things that God intended to be there. Remember, Paul is writing to the saints at Ephesus and to us, today's believers. This isn't written to the world. This is written to believers. Struggles with darkness are not exclusive to the world.

We are not to avoid these things to *become* saints; we are to avoid them because we *are* saints. The call is to be who you already are in Christ. For someone who has received His love, salvation and every spiritual blessing, these things have no rightful place. We cannot have God and hang onto our sin. He is light and in Him there is no darkness at all (1 John 1:5).

Our first response to sin is often simple. We tell ourselves to stop it which sometimes works for a while. If we don't ask God to shed His light on the root causes, we can find ourselves in a cycle.

7. What parts of your life have not been exposed to the Light? Past hurts? Childhood pains? Root causes? Deepest fears? Perpetual struggles? How can you ensure the Light has access to all areas of your life?

Listed along with sexual immorality and impurity is something a little more difficult to recognize, idolatry. It's easy to think that because we aren't physically bowing down to golden calves, we don't struggle with idolatry. *"In times of stress fear and worry, we return to the gods in which we are most familiar trusting."*[xix] This can point us to our idolatries and reveal what areas still need to be surrendered. Without realizing it, we can often supplement God. Idolatry simply stated is anything in our lives that we desire more than God.

8. Is there anything you think you need in addition to God for your life to be okay? Is there anything you desire more than God? *(We know the right answer is "no". Of course we want to only want Jesus. Ask God to shine His light in your heart and give you an honest answer.)*

Being filled with the Spirit is contrasted with being drunk with wine. In both situations, a person operates under the influence of something outside of themselves. Control is being handed over in both cases.

9. Write out Galatians 5:22-23. How is being controlled by the Spirit evidenced in our lives?

We are commanded to live carefully and make the most out of time "because the days are evil." When life speeds up or fills up, prayer and time in the Word are often among the first things to go.

10. Take an honest assessment of how you are spending your time. What is captivating your desires and time more than God right now?

11. The word *Kairos* that is translated "time" means "that which time gives the opportunity to do, and may be necessary but not convenient." What do you feel God prompting you to do that is necessary though perhaps not convenient?

PART 2: NO EXEMPTIONS

READ IT: EPHESIANS 5:21-6:9

22 Wives, submit to your own husbands, as to the Lord. **23** For the husband is the head of the wife even as Christ is the head of the church, his body, and is himself its Savior. **24** Now as the church submits to Christ, so also wives should submit in everything to their husbands. **25** Husbands, love your wives, as Christ loved the church and gave himself up for her, **26** that he might sanctify her, having cleansed her by the washing of water with the word, **27** so that he might present the church to himself in splendor, without spot or wrinkle or any such thing, that she might be holy and without blemish.[u] **28** In the same way husbands should love their wives as their own bodies. He who loves his wife loves himself. **29** For no one ever hated his own flesh, but nourishes and cherishes it, just as Christ does the church,**30** because we are members of his body. **31** "Therefore a man shall leave his father and mother and hold fast to his wife, and the two shall become one flesh." **32** This mystery is profound, and I am saying that it refers to Christ and the church. **33** However, let each one of you love his wife as himself, and let the wife see that she respects her husband.

Children, obey your parents in the Lord, for this is right. **2** "Honor your father and mother" (this is the first commandment with a promise), **3** "that it may go well with you and that you may live long in the land." **4** Fathers, do not provoke your children to anger, but bring them up in the discipline and instruction of the Lord. **5** Bondservants, obey your earthly masters with fear and trembling, with a sincere heart, as you would Christ, **6** not by the way of eye-service, as people-pleasers, but as bondservants of Christ, doing the will of God from the heart,**7** rendering service with a good will as to the Lord and not to man, **8** knowing that whatever good anyone does, this he will receive back from the Lord, whether he is a bondservant or is free. **9** Masters, do the same to them, and stop your threatening, knowing that he who is both their Master[y] and yours is in heaven, and that there is no partiality with him.

UNPACK IT:

- What is the instruction given to wives? What is the motivation? (v.22)
- What instruction is given to husbands? Whose example are they to follow? (v.23-30)
- What is marriage to be a picture of? (v. 23)
- What command is given to children? What is the result? (6:1-2)
- What specific instruction is given to fathers? (v.4)
- What attitude are we to have toward those placed in authority over us? (v.5-7)
- How are those in authority to treat those entrusted to their leadership? (v.9)

WORK IT OUT:

I'm married to a man who is very different from me. I'm extroverted; he is introverted. I always have something to say; he is a great listener. I like to take charge and make things happen; he's much more laid back. I like to think and plan ahead; he prefers not to put the cart before the horse.

You can imagine the early years of our marriage were filled with working out what this submission business looks like. I had many one-sided conversations with God mostly to the effect of, "I don't think this will work in our case" and "Perhaps if we could switch personalities it would work better?" As if the clay should be making suggestions to the Potter? Humility was and is a work in progress!

God in His faithfulness is always teaching me and using any teacher possible. A few years ago He chose to use my dog.

My dog weighs in at about 90 pounds. I have never been much of an animal person but I married a dog lover. As a puppy, he was fairly easy to manage on a walk or run. I could overpower him if necessary, and he would normally comply. One day, we were out for a run and it seemed as though every scent, animal or noise pulled him in the exact opposite direction I was trying to go. He was constantly pulling on the leash. I kept having to stop my run in order to get him back on the path. Because of his sheer size and strength, this was no easy task. It was exhausting (not just the running part) but having a partner who was not so into my agenda. I was very frustrated. Neither one of us was enjoying the run.

As my frustration mounted and my strength faded, God tapped me on the shoulder. I felt as though He was saying something to the effect of, *"How was that for you?"* (and perhaps accompanied by chuckling) and then, *"You can be a little like that sometimes."* Ouch!

God was revealing that submission had little to do with who had the stronger personality or who thought they had the better, carefully thought-out ideas. It was about learning to yield to the authority ordered by God so that our relationship could be enjoyed as He intended. This was a big step of faith for me and very out of my comfort zone.

On another occasion, I was listening to a panel of women discuss how as women, we expect our husbands to love us unconditionally, even when we are difficult to love. But when it comes to showing them respect, we only want to do it when we feel they are worthy of our respect. My eyes were opened wide to the hypocrisy in my own attitude.

Jesus knew this particular thing would be quite difficult for us so He went ahead and modelled exactly what it looked like (Philippians 2:5-7). It wasn't about being any less than who He was, but knowing exactly who He was and what He was called to do.

12. What is your instinctive response to the words *submit* and *respect*?

13. Are there areas in your life where you feel the need to control rather than yield to the authority God has put in place?

14. For some reason, we women seem to struggle with the need to be in control. God has been revealing to me that this need is often rooted in fear. What fears cause you to desire control?

15. List any reasons you can you think of for why we resist being under the control or authority of someone else.

16. Are there any ways you need to surrender control so God can steer your relationship rather than you steering your relationship?

17. Are there any divinely given responsibilities you are neglecting because you are too busy controlling responsibilities He hasn't given you?

Responding in obedience in the relationships God has entrusted to us is one way we show gratitude towards God for what He has done. Andy Stanley describes our human response to God's commands regarding treatment of our spouses like this:

> *"God how can I say thanks? You love me in spite of me. You forgave me. You blessed me. Now what can I do for you? And God responding, 'Go and do the same for your husband or wife, not for their sake but for mine.' Hearing this we might ask, 'Are there any other options? What if I go 11 percent? How about a mission trip?' But God wants us to be the vessels through which He pours His love on our spouses."*[xx]

18. If you are married: Does viewing yourself as a vessel of God's love toward your spouse change your attitude towards the commands given to spouses?

When my nephew was 2, I watched him pace the length of the house while having a conversation on his pretend phone. This was puzzling to me until his dad came home and I saw him do the exact same thing when he received a phone call. Children learn by watching. The next relational command is for children to obey their parents. This is also a call to parents as we are the ones who teach them about obedience. Our lives must display obedience to God in observable ways if we want it to impact our children.

There is no room for public and private persona. Nothing causes children to turn their backs on God and the church faster than hypocrisy. Our most important witness is to our own families.

19. What do your children (or children whom you influence) observe when they look at your life? Do they see the same person on Sunday morning that they see the rest of the week?

My mom tells me there was no more upsetting "compliment" she would receive when my sisters and I were young than, "You're so *lucky*. Your children are so well-behaved!" She wanted to say, "Luck?! You think this is luck? This has been HARD work!" Obedience is a result of discipline and training. We train our children to obey us because one day we want them to obey God. Obedience doesn't equal perfection, for our children or for us. We can be authentic in how we handle mistakes.

Confessing rather than covering: When we lose our temper, or make a wrong decision, we can confess that we made a mistake rather than pretending it wasn't wrong. Growing up, I experienced both of my parents apologizing to me on more than one occasion. I knew that just because they were my parents didn't mean they thought they could do no wrong. There's no need to pretend we are never wrong. It's okay for our kids to know that we are fellow strugglers.

Humbling rather than hiding: My dad told me a story about when I was a teenager. He was driving me home after picking me up very late from school. He asked me what was going on in my life. Apparently my response went something like this: *"You don't even have time for me and now you want to know what's going on in my life?!"* Rather than pretending that it didn't happen, he said that awoke him to the realization that he had been too busy with ministry and needed to spend more time with his family. I'm sure the temptation to pretend it didn't happen was high, but instead he took it as a wake-up call.

Seeking rather than getting stuck: When my dad was sick, I scoured his office for spiritual journals. I was looking for the one written when he was struggling with depression. As I read the pages, it struck me that although he was depressed, he never stopped seeking God and crying out to Him. If our kids see us fight complacency or despair by continuing to seek God, they will be impacted.

20. What would authentic obedience look like to your children (or children whom you influence) in your current stage of life?

21. How can you be intentional about teaching your children to obey you, so that one day they can obey God? Or how can you encourage a parent in your life to be intentional?

SUMMARIZE what God has taught you about intentionally exposing your life to the truth and intentionally obeying Him in relationships:

LIVE UP:

Lord, thank you for giving me the ultimate example of walking in love. You never ask me to do what Jesus didn't model for me. Thank you that I am a dearly loved child and that You gave yourself up for me. Help me to imitate You. Show me if there is any part of my life where I have allowed sexual immorality, impurity, greed, obscenity, foolish talk or coarse joking into my life. I want my standard to be Your unchanging truth, not what my culture says is acceptable. Thank you that when I confess my sin You are faithful and just to forgive my sin and cleanse me from all unrighteousness. Show me how to live as a child of light. I want all areas of my heart, mind and life to be exposed to light because You are Light. Where You are Lord, there is freedom. Show me if anything in me is still in darkness. I cannot discern this on my own. Help me to live carefully. Forgive me for times where I have drifted without intentionally seeking You. Life with You is life to the full and I do not want to miss out on it. Help me to understand Your will so I might not spend life foolishly. Fill me with Your Spirit so my thoughts, words and actions are controlled by You. In whatever measure I work or serve, remind me that You are my audience. I want to work wholeheartedly as if I am working for You and not for men. In the powerful name of Jesus, amen.

Wives: *Thank you that marriage is a picture of Your relationship to the church. Help me to discern any false ideas I have about submission. Give me a heart that desires to respect my husband because it is pleasing to You. Show me where I am resisting this truth in my life. Help him to love me like You love the church. I want our marriage to reflect Your glory and be a light to this dark world. I want to step out in faith and obey You, even if I don't feel like it. Give us a spirit of surrender and selflessness to put each other first.*

Parents: *Help me to see my children as You see them. They are a gift from You and You have placed them in my care. Give me wisdom to teach them Your ways and Your truth. Incline their hearts toward You to want to love and obey You. I need to continually receive Your mercy and grace so I can pass it on to them. Help me to see them as the most valuable gift You have entrusted to me. Protect them from the evil one. Help me to teach them to obey me so one day they may obey You. Help me not to exasperate them to anger, but bring them up in the training and instruction of the Lord.*

---

xvii How People Grow, Dr. Henry Cloud & Dr. John Townsend, p. 99
xviiixviiixviii How People Grow, Dr. Henry Cloud & Dr. John Townsend, p. 103
xix J.D. Greear, Presence, p.56
xx Andy Stanley, iMarriage, p.35-36

WEEK 6: PREPARED FOR BATTLE

READY FOR A FIGHT

For Christmas, my husband bought mini Nerf guns for each member of our family. He thought it might provide some good family fun. On a few occasions, we've set up the playing field. One team of two is stationed in our playroom and the other opposite on the landing. We have makeshift shields set up from larger pieces of furniture that you can take cover behind. My son has play safety goggles from his tool set that we sometimes employ and he also wears his Spiderman mask occasionally for added protection. It's my kind of playing field. It's a controlled atmosphere. There are timeouts to regroup and collect stray bullets and most importantly, there is a place to take cover. If I must participate, this is my preference.

Unfortunately, I haven't always been given the choice of participating. I've also found myself under surprise attack when I least expect it and at inconvenient times. My toddlers think that when I say "Mommy isn't playing right now" or "It's not the designated time for a family nerf fight right now" or "We don't just shoot people!" that I'm trying to be funny. They seem to enjoy the easy target.

This week we are going to study how to be prepared for battle. Walking in love is hard fought and does not come easily. The fight requires us to be prepared. Unfortunately, the enemy doesn't wait until we've set up the playing field. He doesn't play by the rules or pause when we need a time out. He doesn't wait until we have a shelter set up. He's more into the surprise attack when we are most vulnerable.

As you get into the Word this week, we will study how we can walk in the victory that has already been won for us. As you will see, it requires us to be both dependent and active. I'm praying for you!

PART 1: STANDING FIRM

READ IT: EPHESIANS 6:10-13

[10] Finally, be strong in the Lord and in the strength of his might. [11] Put on the whole armor of God, that you may be able to stand against the schemes of the devil. [12] For we do not wrestle against flesh and blood, but against the rulers, against the authorities, against the cosmic powers over this present darkness, against the spiritual forces of evil in the heavenly places. [13] Therefore take up the whole armor of God, that you may be able to withstand in the evil day, and having done all, to stand firm.

UNPACK IT:

- What are we to be strong in? (v.10)
- What are you to *put on* and why? (v.11)
- What do we *not* wrestle against? What *do* we wrestle against? (v.12)
- Where is this battle located? (v.12) What else has taken place there? (1:3, 1:20, 2:6, 3:10)
- What are you to *take up* and why? (v.13)

WORK IT OUT:

The Inescapable Battle: Like it or not, we are in a battle. Stage of life, relationship status, denomination, location, or age does not exempt us from the spiritual battle that rages. It's tempting to think that changing one of those factors will simplify or eliminate the challenges we face but the truth is, the battle rages no matter what. It's not *if or when* we wrestle but that *we wrestle.* We can choose to engage with the victorious side or we can live unaware. Either way, the battle is unavoidable.

1. What are the most difficult people, problems, or circumstances you are currently facing? Are you tempted to think they are the real enemy?

2. Beside your responses to #1, write "NOT THE REAL ENEMY." How does recognizing that the person, problem or circumstance is not the real enemy change your approach to how you "wrestle"?

Whatever challenges you are currently facing are connected to the wrestling match that is taking place in heavenly places. We already know that the enemy comes to steal, kill and destroy (John 10:10) and he would love nothing more than to fly under the radar enough for us to live unaware of the spiritual reality. He wants us to focus our physical resources on what we think are physical problems while leaving the effectual spiritual weapons hanging in the closet.

The Secured Victory: I'm so thankful that the story of our lives is not meant to include the words *severe* and *thumping.* Victory is both secured and ours. We must understand this if we are to live with it as our reality.

In our first week of study, we learned of what has been made available to us in heavenly places including riches, blessings, power and authority. Did the word *might* ring any bells for you? God used His same *great might* to raise Jesus from the dead and seat Him at his right hand in heavenly places (1:19-20).

> *"Power is not a current to be turned on and off. It is a continual, relational, empowering that results from living in Christ. Nor is this power to be used to our personal advantage. The power has one purpose: to enable us to stand with God and against evil."*[xxi]

Thankfully, what is available to us is far greater than what our own strength can provide. We are standing strong in someone so much stronger than ourselves. We are standing in strength that has already been displayed in its fullness and strength that has already been victorious.

1. What two things did God's might accomplish according to Ephesians 1:19-20?

2. What does Jesus Christ have authority over according to Ephesians 1:22-23?

God's might both raised Jesus from the dead and seated Him at His right hand. Can you think of any more victorious place than to be seated beside God Himself? In addition, God placed everything under the authority of Jesus (1:21-22).

> *"In ancient times, being seated was the symbolic posture of a king whose army had already been victorious in battle. Instead of standing, acting, and worrying himself to death, he would park himself on his throne as a visible statement of his complete and utter triumph."*[xxii]

3. According to Ephesians 2:6, who else is seated with Jesus Christ?

When we are told to be strong in the Lord, and in the strength of His might, we are reminded of the irrevocable victory that has already been won. Paul desperately wants us to realize what we already have. Jesus overcame death by the great might of God. He is seated next to God and if we are in Christ Jesus, we are seated with Him. Everything is under His feet. By standing strong in the Lord, we are standing in an already secured victory.

4. How does this truth change your perspective of your current battle?

5. How much power do you think is needed for victory in the battle you may be facing? Is it more than what was required to raise Jesus from the dead?

   I know the answer is "no" but until you say it aloud, it can be easy to think your battle is destined to be a losing one. Remember, the same power lives in us!

The Effectual Weapons: Though the victory is secured, we still have a part to play. We are given two actionable commands to follow if we want to be strengthened in the Lord. Both involve the whole armor of God and both are purposed for standing firm in the inescapable battle.

First of all, we are told to *put on* the whole armor of God, which literally means "to be clothed in." Can you imagine leaving home without clothes? I can't think of anything worse. In this sense, we need to get dressed in the whole armor of God so we can resist the schemes of the enemy.

Schemes is from the word *methodeia* which means *the following or pursuing of orderly and technical procedure in the handling of a subject.*[xxiii]

At first glance, it may seem like the enemy's handiwork is difficult to recognize. As I've paid more attention to my own battles and those I've seen others face, I have found that he has the same basic game plan. Many follow the same pattern, are timed by similar circumstances and present similar temptations. When the schemes are brought into the light, the basic pattern used is easier to recognize. Experiencing victory is connected to our ability to unmask the true enemy behind the battles we face and recognize the attempted deception.

6. What sin or struggles are you most vulnerable to because of fleshly tendencies, innate passions, or desires and weaknesses? What is your greatest area of influence for the kingdom of God?

7. How can being aware of your responses above help you to be on your guard against the schemes of the enemy in your life? Are there any practical ways you can safeguard yourself from being easily baited?

My son has allergies, so I do not leave home without the small plastic bag carrying Benadryl and his Epi pen. No matter what I'm wearing that day or what bag I'm bringing, that small plastic bag gets transferred so it is with me when I'm with him. I never want to be caught in a situation where he needs it and I'm without it. If it needs to be taken up for use, I had better have it with me.

The second instruction we are given is to *take up* the whole armor so that we can withstand the evil day and stand firm. This means to *take something in order to use it.* We *always* need our clothes. We *might* need our supplies. Don't be caught without either!

Next, we will look closer at the effectual weapons and see what we are to wear at all times and what we are to take up and use in the event that we may need it.

PART 2: DRESSED AND READY

READ IT: EPHESIANS 6:10-18

14 Stand therefore, having fastened on the belt of truth, and having put on the breastplate of
righteousness, 15 and, as shoes for your feet, having put on the readiness given by the gospel of peace. 16 In all
circumstances take up the shield of faith, with which you can extinguish all the flaming darts of the evil one; 17 and
take the helmet of salvation, and the sword of the Spirit, which is the word of God, 18 praying at all times in the
Spirit, with all prayer and supplication. To that end keep alert with all perseverance, making supplication for all the
saints,

UNPACK IT:

- What are we to *put on*? (v.15-16)
- What are we to take up and when, and for what purpose? (v.16)
- What other armor are we to take? (v.17)
- What are we to do at all times and for whom? (v.18)

WORK IT OUT:

Standing firm means to be *immovable, unharmed, established, kept intact, to escape in safety, to stand ready or prepared, to be of steadfast mind and a quality of one who does not hesitate or waiver.*[xxiv]

> *"Standing firm is not only about digging in; it's also about moving forward... realize that this armor and these weapons can do more than help you hunker down and white-knuckle it. They can actually dig a stronghold out and advance against the enemy in victory."*[xxv]

I want that to be my reality so desperately, and I bet you do too. The good news is we are told exactly what to do in order for this to become our reality.

The Belt of Truth: The province of Alberta is home to the historical site of the Frank Slide. On April 29, 1903, Turtle Mountain came crashing down in a matter of approximately 100 seconds. One contributing factor to this disaster was that there were many large cracks in the mountain that had filled with water. Over time, the freezing and thawing action of the water widened the cracks creating more instability and setting the stage for the landslide.

Deception works in a similar way. If our minds are not anchored in truth, deceptions can easily fill the cracks. Over time they can expand and create instability in our thinking, reasoning, and convictions. Putting on the full armor of God begins with truth.

Truth is the critical, essential, and foundational element that everything else hangs on. We are to put it on and never be found without it. Other phrases describe the belt of truth as "having girded your loins." For a solider, a girdle was a distinguishing mark. It held together the armor. Everything else hinged on it. With no belt, the tunic could not be tucked into it, the breastplate could not rest on it and the sword could not be carried on it.

The enemy is called the father of lies (John 8:44). In him there is no light or truth. He is a master deceiver, but not overly original. His methodology often follows the same old pattern: "Did God *really* say…?" He hides the consequences in the fine print and has us sign on the dotted line without full disclosure of what sin will cost us. He appeals to our short-sightedness and addiction to sight. He can make temporary and insignificant things seem promising and valuable when the truth is they are empty and very consequential.

8. Have you experienced any consequences of sin that were tucked into the fine print as a result of compromising truth?

9. What does putting on the belt of truth look like in your life?

We must resolve to live by the truth. Begin by exposing your life to the truth, both the Word of God and His Spirit so you know His character and purposes. Merely reading the Bible does not automatically mean it becomes your standard for living. Convictions, responses, attitudes, decisions, and ambitions must be aligned with His standard. Instead of relying on feelings, opinions and the changing culture to determine direction, His truth is the standard everything is filtered through.

10. Have you committed to making God's truth the guiding directive of your life? What is God asking you to do as a result of truth He has revealed?

11. Why is truth so essential to our victory?

The Breastplate of Righteousness: Have you ever left home for a few days and left fruit out on the counter? I have forgotten to put it in the fridge before departing and returned to find fruit flies had set up shop. They didn't need a formal invitation to come. The moist and fermenting environment was invitation enough.

The second part of our uniform to be worn at all times is the breastplate of righteousness. The breastplate protected all the major organs and the protection it offered was the difference between life and death. As the breastplate protects the physical heart, righteousness protects our spiritual heart.

When we choose not to align our behaviour with God's truth, the environment created is welcoming to the enemy. The environment of sin and unrighteousness is the invitation.

12. Are there any attitudes, habits or behaviours in your life that have created an environment where the enemy feels at home?

Truth aligns our thinking with God's standard and righteousness aligns our living. Truth is like the train track and righteousness is choosing to drive the train of our lives on it.[xxvi]

Thankfully, because of Jesus we have been declared righteous before God. We have right standing before God. This is *imputed righteousness*. This is the righteousness that defines us. Jesus in our place. When God looks at us, He sees Jesus for we are hidden in Christ (Colossians 3:3).

There is also *practical righteousness* that we are called to. As you have studied, there are things we are told to put off and put on. Throughout Scripture you will find many more instructions for right living.

13. Is there part of the old self that is difficult for you to put off because it is natural and comfortable? What would be the first step to taking them off so you can put on the new self?

The Holy Spirit is continually chipping away at anything and everything in our lives that doesn't look like Jesus. This wonderful process of sanctification is progressive. As we cooperate with the Holy Spirit, our lives become more practically righteous and we walk protected and in victory because the environment of our life offers no invitation for darkness.

Readiness of the Shoes of the Gospel of Peace: When I taught kindergarten, there was a dad who would occasionally drop his daughter off a few minutes late to one of the other classes. He caught my eye on more than one occasion when he walked by the door because he was wearing socks but no shoes! It was the oddest thing to me. I could never quite figure out how you could leave home without shoes. Shoes seem like a prerequisite for being ready to go anywhere.

14. How does the gospel provide peace in your current battle? How does it make you ready to withstand and push back uncertainty?

We often think of peace as the absence of chaos. My house seems peaceful when it's quiet and tidy which are both rare occasions in this season. But peace is best measured against the backdrop of chaos. When life is not all that we think it should be, we can get an accurate sense of whether or not peace truly rules in us.

When life is characterized by uncertainty, broken-heartedness, disappointment, confusion and instability, and you're not only standing, but still moving forward, you know you are truly fitted with the gospel of peace. The peace of Christ in our minds accompanies the rule of Christ in our hearts.[xxvii]

15. Does your life exhibit peace *with* God in the midst of chaos? What does this say about your current level of trust in Him?

16. Write out Philippians 4:6-7 in the space below. What steps precede the peace of God guarding our hearts and minds?

At all times, we are to be clothed in our spiritual uniform: truth, righteousness, and peace. Next, Paul changes his language and tells us what we are to *take up.*

The Shield of Faith: During my dad's journey with ALS, there were many opportunities to take God at His Word without knowing how it was going to work out in the end. When I look back and remember the difficulty, the anguish, the suffering, the questions, and the emotion, I often wonder how we were brought through that season.

I heard a very timely message only days after the diagnosis that I will never forget. *Always associate the word **faith** with the word **through**. Faith always goes through.*[xxviii] The shield of faith was protection against many flaming arrows the enemy sent in my direction and trust me, there were many. Hard realities were faced, tough questions were left unanswered, and emotional days of anguish were survived. Faith didn't make it *easy*. Faith made it *possible*.

The first thing we are commanded to take up is the shield of faith for the purpose of extinguishing the flaming arrows of the evil one. The shield was large enough that the soldier could be completely protected behind its cover. As much as the other pieces of armor fulfilled their specific tasks of protection, the shield was what made the solider invulnerable. The enemy's purpose in sending flaming arrows as part of an attack was not necessarily to kill, but to distract, divert, and cause chaos.

17. What flaming arrows has the enemy aimed in your direction hoping to catch you without faith as your shield? Worry? Doubt? Fear? Casual familiarity (tempting you to stay only within the limitations of your safety and comfort)?

18. How would taking up the shield of faith extinguish fear, intimitdation, busyness, insecurity, distraction, or discouragement in your life?

Faith is choosing to believe God's Word despite feelings. It is acting like God is telling the truth. It's believing the truth and practicing the righteousness you have been instructed in without knowing how it is going to work out in the end.

19. According to Hebrews 11:6, how necessary is faith in our relationship with God? According to Romans 10:17, where does faith come from? According to James 2:26, what must our faith be combined with?

Faith is absolutely necessary in order to please God. Though He requires it, He has provided a way to have it. God expressed His faithfulness to us in sending Jesus. Jesus displayed His faithfulness by leaving us the Holy Spirit. The Holy Spirit's presence in us allows us to express faithfulness back to God (Galatians 5:22-23).

If you want more faith, you need more of the Word. Faith comes from hearing the Word of God. If you don't know what God has promised and who He is, how will you believe Him? How will you practice an active, present-tense belief that activates resurrection type power in your life if you don't know what you are called to believe? True faith will lead to action. It will lead to acting based on what God has promised and what He says is true. Faith acts like it is true, even if it's hard to believe because God promises the result.

The Helmet of Salvation: In battle, the helmet was the sign of victory. It was the hope. When a solider would've heard the word salvation or saved, they likely would've thought of deliverance from a battle or being carried to a place of victory and safety. The word saved means *entrance into a state of health, wholeness, victory, and safety.*

The brain is so vital to the body's functioning. We rarely engage in activities that pose a threat to our brains without proper protection. The smallest amount of physical damage will reap severe repercussions for the physical body. For this reason, many activities utilize helmets. Should we not protect our minds in the same manner? Our mind is to the soul what the brain is to the body. Imagine the impact of a damaged mind to the soul.

I believe that we can be saved and still miss the opportunity to live in wholeness, victory, and the abundant life that God promises. The enemy is after our minds. Many struggles can be traced back to a vulnerable mind that believed a lie. At some point, there's a good chance the enemy has whispered at least one of the following: *You are unworthy, unloved, incapable, undesirable, unforgivable, unknown, or insignificant.* We possibly have never realized the impact these lies have had on our thinking and living, or we have realized them but never endured the uncomfortable process or letting God uncover, heal, and replace with truth.

20. Have you struggled with any of the thought patterns listed above? How have those thought patterns impacted your feelings, behaviour, and response to truth?

21. How can the truth of the spiritual blessings you have received in Ephesians 1 replace the lies in the above patterns of thinking?

Thankfully, salvation gives us comprehensive coverage. While renewing the mind may sound simple, it is not easy. There is a process we must engage in.

1. Identify thought patterns that you have nursed that are inconsistent with God's truth. It's a sobering thought, but by nursing and rehearsing lies, we have essentially partnered with the enemy!

2. Confess these to the Lord (1 John 1:9).

3. Lastly, we must dismantle lies by taking thoughts captive (2 Corinthians 10:13). This is a continuous and ongoing action. Lies must be replaced with truth at every opportunity. They will come down, but it may take time.

God's Word: The Sword of the Spirit

This is the obvious offensive weapon but it's not really the first mention of it. Truth is based on the Word of God. Righteousness is the application of truth which is based on the Word of God. Peace comes from knowing and trusting God, which comes from standing firm and pressing forward based on truth. Faith comes by hearing the Word of God and is exercised by believing and acting upon the Word of God. All that is made available through salvation is made known to us through the Word of God.

Putting on and taking up the whole armor of God is really all dependent on the Word of God. It is our sword and to be used offensively against the enemy. We put ourselves at dangerous risk if we do not regularly expose our lives to God's Word.

We are to stand firm in what has been done for us, but we cannot do our part if we do not know what God's Word says and how it works.

22. Why is taking up the armor of God dependent on our willingness to access God's Word?

23. Is there anything still hindering you from making exposure to God's Word the priority of your life? What has to change in your belief system in order to view it as critical and irreplacable? How can you make it the priority of your life?

The Secret Weapon: Prayer

"Praying in the Spirit is different from just praying. Most people pray... but most of your prayers tend to be wish lists and prayers for protection. Praying in the Spirit involves engagement with God and assistance from the Spirit that takes us beyond our immediate concerns. True prayer is a comprehensive activity involving a variety of modes from praise to lament, from confession to obedience and from contemplation to intercession. All of life is to be prayed, not just lived. That is why Paul instructs us to pray on all occasions...Prayer is our spiritual breathing." [xxix]

24. Is prayer your first or last resort? Why is this?

25. Do your prayers tend to be wish lists? How can you engage with God in a more comprehensive way?

PART 3: PARTING WORDS

READ IT: EPHESIANS 6:19-24

19 and also for me, that words may be given to me in opening my mouth boldly to proclaim the mystery of the
gospel, 20 for which I am an ambassador in chains, that I may declare it boldly, as I ought to speak. 21 So that you
also may know how I am and what I am doing, Tychicus the beloved brother and faithful minister in the Lord will tell
you everything. 22 I have sent him to you for this very purpose, that you may know how we are, and that he
may encourage your hearts. 23 Peace be to the brothers, and love with faith, from God the Father and the Lord Jesus
Christ. 24 Grace be with all who love our Lord Jesus Christ with love incorruptible.

UNPACK IT:

- For what did Paul request prayer? (v.19)
- For what purpose did Paul send Tychicus? (v.22)
- What did Paul want to remind the Ephesians of in closing? (v.23)
- How did Paul describe the love that accompanied the grace for those who love the Lord? (v.24)

WORK IT OUT:

After explaining to us all that we have received from God, and how to utilize it in order to walk in love victoriously, Paul's last request is for boldness in the gospel. The gospel is the reason why we have access to what Jesus Christ accomplished for us and what enables us to live empowered and free lives. The gospel is the starting point and the continuing, enabling power. Our goal is to know Him and make Him known. As we walk in love the gospel will flow out of us because all of life is the gospel.

26. Take a moment to ask God to give you boldness in the gospel as you speak. Who in your life needs to hear the Good News? Write their names down and ask God to remind you to pray daily for their salvation.

27. Paul sent a messenger to encourage the hearts of the believers much like God still does today. How might God use what He has done in your life to encourage the heart of another?

Paul's final word is that we would be accompanied by grace with a love that is incorruptible, meaning sincere and undiminishing. Most people have heard more religious talk than they have seen real lives transformed by Jesus. The world needs to see lives in Christ lived out before them. People in your life need to see a life in Christ lived out before them. May this be the priority of our hearts: ***To know Him and make Him known.***

WRAP IT UP: TAKING BACK GROUND

Just over a year ago my husband got lost on a hunting trip. He was in unfamiliar woods, snow started falling, and he got turned around. He had no compass, GPS, or consistent cell service, and was walking in a direction that to the best of his knowledge was the right one. Approximately 21 km and 6 hours later he was miraculously found by another group of hunters and safely returned to his group and thankfully to me!

While he had thought he was travelling in the direction of his group, he had spent that time and distance furthering himself from where he was intending to go.

This was particularly odd because he is not the type to get lost. That is completely my department. I can count the number of times he has ever been lost: 1. He was not the one the group was worried about losing. No one was keeping a special eye on him. But walking through a snowstorm in unknown territory with no landmarks or directional indications, his best efforts were useless.

Recently God has been speaking to me about walking in freedom and abundant life. I hadn't thought of myself as someone who was bound by chains so I was a bit surprised when He started revealing areas of my life where I had been an unaware captive.

God was bringing things into the light that needed exposing through a Bible study I was doing. These were not obvious destructive habits that anyone could've pointed out. Many of them were subtle. They were small areas where something untrue had taken root and naturally, consequences had followed.

There were parts of my personality and self-perception that had been damaged by the criticism of others. They were misdirected things about me that I felt were wrong and mistakes rather than things God wanted to use in his kingdom. There were areas that were wrongly motivated and where gifts had been misapplied.

Much like my husband, these were not areas I was intentional about getting lost in. It just happened. It's easy in this world to get turned around. Many of us come to a point of salvation in Christ but never allow God into past hurts. We never pull out the contents of the closet and let God sort through what is true and what isn't.

We don't look at who He made us and how we haven't been able to be used fully of Him. The process can be uncomfortable and time consuming at best and painful at worst.

Sometimes we can lose ground in our lives and not even be aware of it. How can we stand firm against the enemy and push forward when we are bound by chains?

My journey of learning to walk in love began with God revealing that I didn't have the good grasp I thought I did on what He wanted for me and from me. I've realized that God wants me on offense as well as defense. There's ground in my life that has been lost that He wants to take back. But this will not happen simply because I have a good sense of direction (which I don't). This will happen by standing firm in what has already been done for me and putting on and taking up the full armor of God. It's the only way to stand and the only way to have complete access to ongoing victory.

I want victory. I want abundant life. I want to walk in love. And I want to be prepared and unhindered for the hard fought battle that I know it will always be.

SUMMARIZE what you have learned about the battle:

LIVE UP:

Use the space below to write out your own strategic prayer based on the scripture that you studied this week. Each of the previous weeks of "Live Up" were written based on the scripture studied. To do this, go to the beginning of the passage (6:10) and write each verse out as a specific request for your life. There's no better way to start praying in the Spirit than to agree with what He commands and ask for what He already wants to give you. Get writing!

xxi NIV Application Commentary Ephesians, Klyne Snodgrass, p.346
xxii The Armor of God, Priscilla Shirer, p.20
xxiii The Hebrew Greek Key Study Bible, Lexical Aids to the New Testament, 3180-Methodeia
xxiv Blueletterbible.org, "Histemi"
xxv The Armor of God, Priscilla Shirer, p.114-115
xxvi The Armor of God, Priscilla Shirer
xxvii Living Beyond Yourself, Beth Moore
xxviii Living Beyond Yourself, Beth Moore
xxixNIV Application Commentary Ephesians, Klyne Snodgrass, p.359

VIDEO SESSION VIEWER GUIDES

SESSION 1: WHO I AM

Video Session 1 is available at everydaytruth.ca/ephesians

Open your Bible to Ephesians 1:3 (ESV) and read along

WALKING IN LOVE BEGINS WITH ______________ WHO I AM

1. He ________ ______________ my ____________

2. My ____________ is ______________

3. I will ______________ to __________ into my identity

Fill in the Blank Answers: alone, determined, identity, identity, secure, continue, grow

REFLECTION/DISCUSSION QUESTIONS:

To be used following the video with a small group, a friend, or for reflection if you're participating alone.

1. Have you known someone who has modelled a life of love? Describe what you have seen demonstrated in his or her life.

2. The term "walk" used in Ephesians is meant to describe all of life. It's how you conduct yourself in every area with exemption or exception. Currently, which picture better describes your relationship with God: One of many compartments? Or a permeating force affecting everything?

3. What do you currently feel defined by? Past mistakes? A specific role? Your abilities or accomplishments? A relationship or lack of one? A struggle? A circumstance? A tragedy?

Read Ephesians 1 aloud whether you're reflecting alone or discussing with a group. It might seem like a lot, but I promise it'll take just a few minutes. Go ahead... read away!

4. Are there any circumstances or relationships you have experienced that have influenced you toward either *believing* or *doubting* who you are in Christ?

5. We need to be defined by the truth that we are HIS. Look back at your answer to #3. Does this support or contradict the identity description found in Ephesians 1?

6. Are you currently facing any obstacles to believing and living as though you have every spiritual blessing?

WARM UP:

- What was your biggest take away from studying Ephesians 1?

- Read Matthew 7:24-27 and Ephesians 1:18-20 and finish this sentence: *My present tense level of BELIEF is like [sand, water, rock, grass, gravel, other] because...*

SESSION 2: HIS GREAT LOVE

Video Session 2 is available at everydaytruth.ca/ephesians

Open your Bibles to Ephesians 2:4-10 and read along (we are reading from ESV)

WALKING IN LOVE __________ AS I UNDERSTAND __________ I HAVE BEEN LOVED

1. He loved me when there was __________ __________ about me.

2. He loved me because of __________

3. He loves me with great __________

   Restoration is a lifelong process. As He does His restoring work in our lives, He wants to use us as restoration tools in the lives of others.

4. He loved me enough to __________ His only Son to bring me __________ to Himself

Fill in the Blank Answers: flows, how, nothing, lovable, Himself, purpose, sacrifice, back

REFLECTION/DISCUSSION QUESTIONS:

To be used following the video individually for reflection, or for discussion with a friend or small group.

1. Describe a time when you've received mercy. How did you feel? How did you respond to it?

Read Ephesians chapter 2 aloud whether you're reflecting alone or discussing with a group.

2. How does Paul's description of your condition challenge your view of yourself?

3. *"The same mercy and grace that saved me can save anyone."* We've all come from the same place. We were plucked from a state of death when God saved us. How does understanding this level ground empower you to be merciful towards people who don't know Jesus, or who are starting out in their walk with Him?

4. Have you experienced the riches of God's mercy in your life or do you view Him as waiting to pounce and punish?

5. Does understanding "this is NOT your own doing" in terms of your salvation change how freely you share the gospel? (2:8)

6. Are you able to see the "masterpiece" (God's original intent) in yourself and in others or are you easily distracted by the "mud" (sin, struggles, behaviour etc.)?

7. Are you tempted to view the good works certain people do as more important than others?

8. *"The call of God on our lives is about obedience."* Have you been tempted to busy yourself with work He's called other's to do, or have you set out with the primary goal of obeying whatever He specifically asks of you?

9. Do you view yourself as being at peace with God and reconciled to Him, or do you still live feeling like He is hostile towards you?

WARM UP:

- What was your biggest take away from your study of Ephesians 2?

SESSION 3: THE MAIN THING

Video Session 3 is available at everydaytruth.ca/ephesians

Open your Bibles to Ephesians 3:7-10 and read along (we are reading from ESV)

WALKING IN LOVE IS THE ________________

1. If you have __________ the gospel, you are now a ____________ of the gospel

2. As you receive __________________, you are made a minister of ____________

3. As you are __________ and ___________ in love, you will be the _______________

Fill in the Blank Answers: gospel, received, minister, grace, grace, rooted, grounded, the gospel,

REFLECTION/DISCUSSION QUESTIONS:

To be used following the video individually for reflection, or for discussion with a friend or small group.

1. Which tree better reflects your approach to spiritual life? A Christmas tree or a cherry tree?

2. How can you change your focus from performance to connection?

Read Ephesians 3:1-20 aloud.

3. Think about what the gospel means to you. Jot down 3 words that reflect what it means to you personally.

4. Read 1 Corinthians 15:1-4 and write a scriptural definition of the gospel.

5. For you, was the gospel only the entry for your salvation, or is it the reality that you continually live in?[xxx]

6. Do you see yourself as a minister of the gospel? Why or why not?

7. What gifts of grace has God ministered to you that you've been able to pass on to others? Describe how you felt.

8. Do you view ministering to people as pouring yourself out, or a way that God also pours in to you?

9. The Christian life was meant to bring freedom but often we view it as being restrictive. What is most challenging to you about being a Christian? How might a deeper understanding of the gospel change your outlook?

10. What distracts you from Jesus on a day to day basis?

WARM UP:

- What was your biggest take away from your study of Ephesians 3?

SESSION 4: THE MIRROR

Video Session 4 is available at everydaytruth.ca/ephesians

Open your Bibles to Ephesians 4:1-7 and read along (we are reading from ESV)

WALKING IN LOVE IS A ____________________ OF A ______________ RELATIONSHIP.

1. A loving relationship will ____________________ a ________________ to live ________________ of the call

2. A loving relationship gives us a ____________________ part in the body

3. A loving relationship will ____________________ sanctify you

Fill in the Blank Answers: reflection, loving, ignite, desire, worthy, purposeful, continually,

REFLECTION/DISCUSSION QUESTIONS:

To be used following the video individually for reflection, or for discussion with a friend or small group.

1. *The calling you have received is the divine invitation to embrace the salvation of God and to respond to His grace in obedience.* Are there truths that have filled your heart to overflowing from your study of the first half of Ephesians? In three words, summarize what God has spoken to you about so far. Is there anything still standing between you and embracing all God has made available?

Read Ephesians 4:1-32 aloud whether you're reflecting alone or discussing with a group.

2. The qualities mentioned by Paul will characterize our lives as we receive all He has made available. Why is walking in love only possible when you are presently and continuously walking with God?

3. *What He does in my life is not only for my benefit.* Reflect on your own life story: What challenges and revealed truths have marked your spiritual journey? Who do you feel burdened for? What are you passionate about? What has God delivered you from? How might God want to use your story to encourage and impact the lives of others?

4. The process of putting off the old and putting on the new is bridged by the renewing of the mind. How has God renewed your mind? How can you intentionally position yourself so your mind is available for renewal?

What tools has God used to sanctify you? Is there anything that can be changed in your life so you can better cooperate with this ongoing process?

WARM UP:

- What was your biggest take away from your study of Ephesians 4?

SESSION 5: NOT BY ACCIDENT

Video Session 5 is available at everydaytruth.ca/ephesians

Open your Bibles to Ephesians 5:15-17 and read along (we are reading from ESV)

WALKING IN LOVE IS ________________ ________________

1. We need to be intentional about ________________ our lives to the ______________
2. We need to be intentional about ________________ God in our ________________

Fill in the Blank Answers: living, intentionally, exposing, truth, obeying, relationships,

REFLECTION/DISCUSSION QUESTIONS:

To be used following the video individually for reflection, or for discussion with a friend or small group.

1. *When travelling in unfamiliar territory, without careful attention to direction, and progress being made, you will never arrive at the destination.* When have you lived intentionally or carefully? When have you felt more like a drifting boat? Explain.

2. When we do not live intentionally, we can slowly lose ground without realizing it. Can you identify any areas of your life that have been fallen prey to the "slow fade"?

Read Ephesians 5:1-6:9 aloud whether you're reflecting alone or discussing with a group.

3. *Time is a valuable resource. We can always find time for the things we deem important.* What currently occupies the majority of your free time? Do you find yourself saying, "I don't have time" when it comes to spiritual disciplines? What can you rearrange in your life in order to prioritze exposing your life to truth?

4. *Our relationship with God will always manifest itself in our relationships with others.* Are there any relationships in which you struggle to obey God? What is the difference between acting in faith (obeying even when you don't see how it will work) and acting fake (loving when you don't feel like it)?

Which best describes your current reality: Disobedient? Obedience from discipline? Obedience from desire? Or obedience from delight? How might a person transition from disobedience to obedience born from delighting in God?

WARM UP:

- What was your biggest take away from your study of Ephesians 5?

SESSION 6: HARD FOUGHT

Video Session 6 is available at everydaytruth.ca/ephesians

Open your Bible to Ephesians 6:10-13 and read along (we are reading from ESV).

WALKING IN LOVE IS A ____________________

- The battle is inescapable
- The weapons are effectual
- The victory is secured

Our Spiritual Uniform: Meant to be worn at ALL times

1. Belt of ______________: THE standard that we measure everything against in our lives

2. Breastplate of ____________________ : Upright living that aligns with God's standards

3. Readiness given by the gospel of __________________ (shoes)

4. Shield of _____________: Faith is what fills the gap between what we can see with our own perspective and the truth of God's Word

5. Helmet of _________________: Eternally in heaven and our liberation in this life

6. Sword of the Spirit: The _____________ of _______________ (our ____________ offensive weapon)

The thing that continually empowers the armor is _____________________ at _________ times

Fill in the Blank Answers: battle, truth, righteousness, peace, faith, salvation, Word, God, only, praying, all

REFLECTION/DISCUSSION QUESTIONS:

To be used following the video individually for reflection, or for discussion with a friend or small group.

1. Does your spiritual story thus far read as one of victory or defeat?

2. Is your spiritual mindset more offensive or defensive in nature? Intimdated or victorious? One of surviving or thriving?

3. What picture comes to mind when you hear, "Stand firm!"? Does it include pressing forward? Why or why not?

Read Ephesians 6:10-24 aloud whether you're reflecting alone or discussing with a group.

4. *"The battle is inescapable. The weapons are effectual. The victory is secure."* Which part of this statement is most challenging for you to believe in your day-to-day living: there is always a battle raging, that the armor of God works, or that God has already won the victory?

5. Is there any part of your spiritual uniform (truth, righteousness, or peace) you have not been in the habit of wearing consistently that has left you vulnerable?

6. Which of the weapons we are called to "take up" are you the most and least comfortable putting to use?

7. Why are all the pieces of the armor so essential to take up together? Is there any one piece that is more difficult for you to take up?

8. How can you be both an offensive and defensive spiritual player, pushing back darkness and advancing the kingdom?

[xxx] Gospel Revolution, J.D. Greear,

WARM UP:

What was your biggest takeaway from your study of Ephesians 6?

SESSION 7: WALKING IN LOVE

Video Session 7 is available at everydaytruth.ca/ephesians

- Walking in love begins with ______________ ________ ____ ________
- Walking in love________ as I understand ________ I have been ________
- Walking in love is the ________
- Walking in love is a ______________ of a ______________ relationship
- Walking in love is ______________ __________________
- Walking in love is a ________________

REFLECTION/DISCUSSION QUESTIONS:

To be used following the video individually for reflection, or for discussion with a friend or small group.

1. Walking in love is to encompass and affect all of life. What areas of your life have been most affected as you've studied Ephesians?

2. Do you view spiritual growth more like the growth of a tree or an extreme makeover show? Which do you think is a more realistic picture of spiritual growth and why?

3. Has your understanding deepended or changed in the following areas?
    a. Who you are in Christ? What implications has this had on your life?

    b. God's love for you? If so, how?

    c. The gospel?

    d. Has your motivation for obedience to God changed? How so?

    e. Your intentions? Priorities?

4. Has God opened up your eyes to the spiritual reality behind a current challenge? How have you exchanged physical weapons for spiritual ones? What difference has this made?

5. Are you putting on and taking up the full armor of God? Are there any areas of your life that are unprotected and vulnerable to spiritual attack?

6. John 15:5 reminds us that apart from Jesus Christ, we can do nothing. What would you like to see God do in your life that you know you can't already do on your own?

REFLECT, REMEMBER & RESPOND:

HOW HAS GOD MARKED YOUR LIFE? WRITE IT DOWN AND RESPOND BELOW.

"BE TRANSFORMED BY THE RENEWING OF YOUR MIND." (ROMANS 12:2)

www.ingramcontent.com/pod-product-compliance
Ingram Content Group UK Ltd.
Pitfield, Milton Keynes, MK11 3LW, UK
UKHW062009290726
14090UKWH00022B/1473